OIL AND DEVELOPMENT IN THE MIDDLE EAST

David G. Edens

OIL AND DEVELOPMENT IN THE MIDDLE EAST

PRAEGER PUBLISHERS
Praeger Special Studies

New York • London • Sydney • Toronto

Library of Congress Cataloging in Publication Data

Edens, David G
   Oil and development in the Middle East.

   Includes bibliographical references.
   1. Petroleum industry and trade--Near East--
Finance. 2. Near East--Economic conditions.
3. Near East--Social conditions. I. Title.
HD9576.N36E33   330.9'56'04   79-868
ISBN 0-03-049141-X

PRAEGER PUBLISHERS
PRAEGER SPECIAL STUDIES
383 Madison Avenue, New York, N.Y. 10017, U.S.A.

Published in the United States of America in 1979
by Praeger Publishers,
A Division of Holt, Rinehart and Winston, CBS, Inc.

9   038   987654321

To SJE

PREFACE

A witticism about Saudi Arabia a decade or so ago was that the kingdom was leaping headlong from the twelfth into the sixteenth century. In the new era of high-priced oil, this interpretation is obsolete; in some respects, Saudi Arabia is moving into the twenty-first century, while, in others, it is still mired in traditionalism. This uneven pattern of development is representative of the other Middle Eastern oil states and is evident to a lesser degree in the other Middle Eastern countries as well, as all are experiencing the stresses that accompany imbalanced social change.*

Thinly populated oil states have abundant capital, while the larger, more densely populated countries, relying on traditional agriculture and trade for income, face chronic capital shortages and foreign payments deficits. Manufacturing, aside from petroleum-related activities, is underdeveloped, and economic structures remain lopsided. Aside from Israel, modern skills are scarce relative to the population, but they are most conspicuously lacking in the capital-rich oil states. Natural conditions and human foibles contribute to these problems. An adverse climate and inelastic supplies of arable land make growth in agricultural productivity slow and costly. Further, rapid population growth impedes human resource development and capital formation by stimulating present consumption. Military spending complicates the process of redressing factor imbalances by draining away resources that otherwise might be used for investment in equipment or in the creation of skills. The tendency toward excessive centralization of decision making constrains innovation and hampers the technological adaptation needed for viable industrial development.

Since the oil price revolution, the process of redressing the region's imbalances has accelerated. Capital is flowing from the oil states to the poorer states, while the flow of labor from the poorer states to the oil states has increased. Even so, the general scarcity of modern skills means that redressing the region's factor-imbalance problem will probably be expensive and time consuming.

In studying these varied topics, the difficulties of inadequate statistical information are magnified by the large geographic size of

---

*By development, I mean structural and institutional changes that increase worker productivity and improve the incomes of the lower economic classes, while widening the range of choice for all.

the study area. There is no universally accepted boundary definition of the Middle East, except that the term usually includes the area of southwest Asia lying between the USSR and the Indian Ocean. The definition used here includes the southwest Asian countries of Bahrain, Iran, Iraq, Israel, Jordan, Kuwait, Lebanon, Oman, the People's Republic of Southern Yemen, Qatar, Saudi Arabia, Syria, Turkdy, and the Republic of Yemen. In addition, the definition includes the northeast African states of Libya, the Sudan, and Egypt, as well as the Maghreb, or northwest African states of Algeria, Morocco, and Tunisia. As the data permit, the United Arab Emirates is included. Pakistan and Afghanistan, sometimes considered to be part of the Middle East, are excluded.

It should be emphasized at the outset that the statistics pertaining to Middle Eastern economies are subject to error, in some cases in excess of plus or minus 10 percent. Some distortion probably is deliberate, as governments may use reported statistics for purposes of national aggrandizement or military strategy or in order to disguise economic problems. Furthermore, economic statistics are usually the by-products of other government or business activity and often have been collected by persons other than trained statistical workers. With these conditions in mind, the data have been carefully evaluated and screened before being used here. When more than one source was available, comparisons were made and the most plausible data adopted for use.

As the work relies heavily on statistics published by the international agencies, the uneven appearance of data through time also presents a problem. Financial statistics appear within a few months, whereas information on population characteristics, the labor force, and land use may be many years out-of-date. Under these circumstances, every effort has been made to bring the time series into the mid-1970s (1974-76), and, except in a few unavoidable instances, this objective has been achieved.

Inevitably, the limitations of the data have shaped the format of this book. There are important topics that have not been covered and others that have been treated only partially because of the inadequacy of available information. At the risk of overgeneralization, inferences have been drawn, in some cases, from a few sets of circumstances or examples in order to reach tentative conclusions about the area at large. Thus, the work cannot be a final or complete analysis of Middle Eastern economic development. Rather, by looking at the region as a whole, its aim is to analyze some of the patterns of development that have become clear thus far.

I wish to thank my colleagues Morris Singer, Imanuel Wexler, and Stephen Miller for their constructive criticism of an earlier draft of this book. Comments by Nazem Abdalla and Mahmud Faksh have also been helpful. I am particularly indebted to Charles Issawi and the late Phillip Taylor for their encouragement and for sharing their knowledge of Middle Eastern economic conditions. Finally, special thanks go to Sandra Edens for her steadfast moral support and her editorial judgment. Needless to say, any remaining errors or misinterpretations are mine.

CONTENTS

LIST OF TABLES AND FIGURES

LIST OF ABBREVIATIONS, ACRONYMS, AND COMPANY NAMES

Amoseas	Standard Oil of California and Texaco
APOC	Ango-Persian Oil Company
Aramco	Arabian American Oil Company
BP	British Petroleum Company
c.i.f.	cost, insurance, and freight
DAC	Development Assistance Committee
Exxon	Standard Oil Company of New Jersey
FAO	Food and Agricultural Organization of the United Nations
FLN	National Liberation Front
ICOR	incremental capital/output ratio
IEA	International Energy Agency
IMF	International Monetary Fund
IPC	Iraq Petroleum Company
KOC	Kuwait Oil Company
mer	maximum efficient rate of flow
OAPEC	Organization of Arab Petroleum Exporting Countries
OBU	Offshore Banking Unit
OECD	Organization of Economic Cooperation and Development
OPEC	Organization of Petroleum Exporting Countries
R&D	research and development
SONATRACH	Societe Nationale de Transport et de Commercialisation
Texaco	Texas Company
UNESCO	United Nations Educational, Scientific, and Cultural Organization

OIL AND
DEVELOPMENT IN
THE MIDDLE EAST

1

FACTOR PROPORTIONS

The salient economic characteristic of the Middle East today is the extreme variation in factor proportions among the countries of the area. At the present time, nonhuman wealth is predominantly in the form of oil reserves, but these are unevenly distributed. In most of the area, arable land and human skills are scarce in relation to population. This disproportion of wealth and population results in great disparity in per capita incomes and patterns of development, so that economic advance for the region, as a whole, depends on general improvement in resource proportions. Although the oil price revolution of the 1970s increased inequality in the distribution of income and wealth, it provided the first real opportunity in the modern era for closing the economic gap between the region and the industrial world.

HUMAN RESOURCES

Populations of Middle Eastern countries are relatively small to medium sized, as none exceeds 40 million, and some are no larger than a few hundred thousand. (See Table 1.1.) In the period since World War II, populations have been growing rapidly. Natural rates of increase exceed 3 percent a year in several states, and new immigration serves to lift rates of increase to unusually high levels in others, notably in the Gulf region. Middle Eastern growth rates can be seen in perspective by observing that the population of the world at large has grown at the rate of 1.9 percent since 1950, while the mature, industrial societies have grown at only 1.0 percent a year.

Participation in economic activity is unusually limited in the area.* Nature discourages industrial development in the Middle East, and traditional agriculture represents endless struggle against relentlessly unrewarding natural conditions. Meager returns for effort expended in agriculture provide little incentive to offer labor services beyond the point at which subsistence requirements are satisfied; therefore, institutional arrangements for managing scarcity have evolved.

The most pervasive among these is the extended family, the purpose of which is to provide distributive justice by apportioning shares in static incomes over all family members. In the traditional culture of the area, the family is the basic social unit to which the individual members are subordinate. Headed by the senior male, it includes all of his sons and their wives and children, as well as unmarried daughters and granddaughters. This structure is basically the same among nomad and settled peoples, although it is losing its importance in the larger cities.

The extended family, consisting of perhaps several dozen members, can be found living in close proximity in clusters of tents in the desert or in a single house or a compound in towns. The family divides and reallocates its members when the elder male dies, and each son becomes the head of a new and distinct extended family unit. This process has withstood the passage of time and remains a basic feature of the social fabric of the area. The extended family holds capital assets in common, whether they take the form of livestock among the Bedouin or fixed capital of the enterprise at which the members work. Wage earnings are pooled, and household expenses are met from the common fund. Women may tend the herds or work in the fields of their families; otherwise, their activities are confined to the household.[1]

These arrangements restrict both male and female participation in economic activity, as the pooling of wealth and income tends to weaken the connection between personal effort and reward. On the one hand, the institution has value as a social welfare system in that no widow or child will be without protection, but, on the other, it provides a disincentive to expend effort, which is reflected in lower participation rates than would otherwise be the case. The extended family thus contributes to security at the expense of productivity.

---

*Participation rates in the Middle East are, in most cases, 30 percent or less. Elsewhere, rates may range from 40 to 50 percent. In black Africa, for example, the mean of participation rates is 44 percent. In Europe, the mean is 42 percent; and in Southeast Asia, it is 38 percent.

TABLE 1.1

Population Characteristics, Middle Eastern Countries, Mid-1970s

Country	1974 Population (millions)	Rates of Population Growth, 1965-74	Economically Active Population as Percent of Total	Population per Square Kilometer of Total Area
Major oil states				
Algeria	15.18	3.3	19	7
Iran	33.10	3.0	31	20
Iraq	10.77	3.8	29	25
Kuwait	0.93	7.8	32	52
Libya	2.24	3.7	21	1
Oman	0.75	3.1	25	3
Qatar	0.19	8.5	—	9
Saudi Arabia	5.42	2.9	29	3
United Arab Emirates	0.34	17.1	—	4
Other states				
Bahrain	0.25	3.3	28	404
Egypt	36.35	2.4	25	36
Israel	3.30	3.0	34	159
Jordan	2.62	3.6	23	27
Lebanon	3.07	2.9	27	295
Morocco	16.29	3.6	26	36
Northern Yemen	6.40	2.4	—	33
Southern Yemen	1.63	3.1	—	6
Sudan	17.53	2.6	31	7
Syria	7.18	3.3	24	39
Tunisia	5.64	2.3	29	34
Turkey	38.85	2.3	41	50

Sources: International Bank for Reconstruction and Development, World Bank Atlas, 1976 (Washington, D.C.: IBRD, 1976); International Bank for Reconstruction and Development, World Tables, 1975 (Washington, D.C.: IBRD, 1976); United Nations, Demographic Yearbook, 1975 (New York: United Nations, 1976); and International Labour Office, Year Book of Labour Statistics, 1974 (Geneva: ILO, 1974). The estimate for Saudi Arabia is based on census data, found in Central Department of Statistics, Census of Population, 1382-3 (Riyadh, Kingdom of Saudi Arabia: Ministry of Finance and National Economy, 1964), adjusted for undercounting and extrapolated to 1974.

The traditional system also contributes to high illiteracy rates, as the subordinate position of women tends to ensure their undereducation. Female illiteracy rates are, with a few exceptions, in excess of 80 percent. Unusually high rates of female illiteracy serve to raise average rates. (See Table 1.2.) Although they are generally well below those of female rates, male illiteracy rates are 50 percent or greater in most parts of the region.

Substantial adult illiteracy imposes a serious constraint on the ability of the labor force to acquire the technical skills necessary for modern economic development, and, in most countries, it is necessary to establish high levels of enrollment in primary education before substantial progress can be made toward solving the area's skill shortages internally (through professional and technical training later on). Upgrading the quality of the indigenous labor force is thus a long-term proposition. In general, the problems of illiteracy and skill deficiency are more acute among the oil states than among the others, where, in several cases, modern education is well established.

Despite their vastly higher-income levels, the quality of life, in general, is not proportionately higher among the affluent oil states than elsewhere. Aside from energy consumption, the indicators of living standards are not impressively different. Among both the oil states and the others, caloric supplies are typically less than standard requirements, and, in general, per capita protein supplies are substantially less than in the more developed countries and the world at large. As average measures do not reflect distributional inequalities and as the upper-income classes in most Middle Eastern countries are likely to be well nourished, the poorer classes in both oil and non-oil states must be rather seriously malnourished.

Using hospital beds as an indication of medical services, the oil states are only marginally better supplied in this socially important area than are the others. Medical services are particularly scarce in the south Arabian states, Syria, and the Sudan, while a serious shortage of doctors exists everywhere in the Middle East except in Israel and Kuwait. (See Table 7.9.) Reflecting these and similar limitations, life expectancy at birth rarely exceeds 55 years. (See Table 1.3.)

The population characteristics that have emerged include rapid growth, low rates of participation in economic activity, high rates of illiteracy, and indications of nutritional deficiencies. These findings indicate some serious human resource problems that will have to be solved if modern development is to be facilitated in the area. Under prevailing conditions, the costs of rapid population growth are manifold. Given the prevalence of low participation in economic activity, rapid population growth serves to raise the burden of dependency carried by those equipped to work. At the same time, it overloads rudimentary education systems, thus compounding the difficulty involved

TABLE 1.2

Some Indicators of Living Standards, Middle Eastern Countries, 1970s

Country	Per Capita Caloric Supply (percent of requirement)	Illiterate as Percent of Adult Population	Energy Consumption per Capita (kilograms coal equivalent)	Population per Hospital Bed	1974 per Capita GNP (U.S. dollars)
Major oil states					
Algeria	80	75	674	334	648
Iran	86	63	1,058	673	1,060
Iraq	93	74	724	525	966
Kuwait	—	45	10,886	197	11,645
Libya	108	67	5,727	206	3,362
Oman	—	93	181	206	1,240
Qatar	—	79	12,611	2,536	5,842
Saudi Arabia	86	85	1,640	206	3,080
United Arab Emirates	—	79	8,781	560	13,500
Other states					
Bahrain	—	60	4,569	430	2,245
Egypt	94	60	294	236	278
Israel	116	12	2,844	461	3,380
Jordan	94	55	339	169	397
Lebanon	96	14	870	753	1,077
Morocco	99	76	222	254	426
Northern Yemen	84	85	13	677	116
Southern Yemen	91	90	404	1,452	123
Sudan	102	81	123	1,152	146
Syria	86	60	465	1,108	485
Tunisia	110	68	368	1,013	546
Turkey		45	615	490	690

Note: To reduce distortions caused by under- or overvaluation of currencies, the World Bank uses a multiyear base period method for converting local currency gross national product (GNP) to current dollars. In this case, local currency GNPs were expressed in weighted average 1972-74 prices and then converted to 1972-74 dollars at the average GNP-weighted exchange rates for the period. The results were linked to current 1974 dollars by the U.S. GNP deflator. Although this method dampens the income effect of the oil price increases of 1973, the data remain the best available for the purposes of international comparison.

Sources: International Bank for Reconstruction and Development, World Tables, 1975 (Washington, D.C.: IBRD, 1976); and United Nations, Statistical Yearbook, 1974 (New York: United Nations, 1975). The GNP figures used to estimate 1974 per capita income are from International Bank for Reconstruction and Development, World Bank Atlas, 1975 (Washington, D.C.: IBRD, 1975).

TABLE 1.3

Indicators of Income, Resources, and Development, Middle Eastern Countries, 1970s

Country	Income	Nonhuman Resources		Human Resources		Development			
	1974 per Capita GNP (U.S. dollars)	1974 Oil Reserves per Capita (metric tons)	Arable and Cropped Land per Capita (acres)	Literate as Percent of Population (age 15 and over)	Professionals and Technicians as Percent of Labor Force	Industry's Share in GDP	Industry's Share in Labor Force	Gross Reproduction Rate	Life Expectancy at Birth
Major oil states									
United Arab Emirates	13,500	13,610.5	0.15	21	—	—	—	—	—
Kuwait	11,645	11,948.2	0.00	55	10.7	73	34	3.6	64
Qatar	5,842	4,308.2	0.03	21	—	—	—	—	—
Libya	3,362	1,620.1	2.88	33	3.1	68	22	3.3	52
Saudi Arabia	3,080	4,357.5	0.41	15	4.8	79	28	3.5	42
Oman	1,240	1,091.4	0.12	7	—	—	—	—	—
Iran	1,060	272.0	1.24	37	2.7	59	24	3.4	50
Iraq	966	443.4	1.19	26	3.4	46	10	3.5	53
Algeria	648	69.2	1.14	25	—	44	13	3.5	52
Other states									
Israel	3,380	0.1	0.32	88	16.5	37	34	1.8	72
Bahrain	2,245	187.1	0.02	40	8.0	75	34	1.9	58
Lebanon	1,077	0.0	0.29	86	9.2	21	24	2.6	55
Turkey	690	1.7	1.84	55	3.2	31	12	3.1	56
Tunisia	546	26.6	2.04	32	4.0	27	19	3.5	55
Syria	485	28.5	2.09	40	4.3	23	18	3.4	50
Morocco	426	0.0	1.16	24	4.0	27	15	3.5	54
Jordan	397	0.0	1.26	45	4.0	21	16	3.0	53
Egypt	278	13.9	0.20	40	4.4	27	3	3.4	48
Sudan	146	0.0	1.03	19	—	15	—	3.5	42
Southern Yemen	123	0.0	0.40	10	—	11	—	—	—
Northern Yemen	116	0.0	0.48	15	—	—	—	—	—

Sources: International Bank for Reconstruction and Development, World Bank Atlas, 1975 (Washington, D.C.: IBRD, 1975); "Worldwide Report," Oil and Gas Journal 72, no. 52 (December 30, 1974): 108-9; Food and Agricultural Organization of the United Nations, Production Yearbook, 1974 (Rome: FAO, 1975); International Labour Organization, Yearbook of Labour Statistics, 1974 (Geneva: ILO, 1974); United Nations Yearbook of National Accounts Statistics (New York: United Nations), various issues; International Bank for Reconstruction and Development, World Tables, 1975 (Washington, D.C.: IBRD, 1976); and United Nations Educational, Scientific and Cultural Organization, Statistical Yearbook, 1974 (Paris: UNESCO, 1975). The estimate of industry's share in the labor force in Saudi Arabia is drawn from Central Planning Organization, Development Plan 1390 A.H. (Riyadh: Government of Saudi Arabia, 1970). Estimates for the North African countries are from Economic Commission for Africa, Summaries of Economic Data (Addis Ababa, Ethiopia: ECA), various issues.

in spreading literacy. It also tends to worsen the proportions between human and other resources, particularly land, which is relatively inelastic in supply.

AGRICULTURAL RESOURCES

At the present time, only Bahrain and Lebanon are densely settled in terms of population per square kilometer of total area. (See Table 1.1.) By this measure, the Middle East in general appears to be underpopulated in relation to Europe and the Far East. Densities per square kilometer of total area, however, are poor indicators of resource proportions. Population per square kilometer of arable and cropped land is a far more significant measure of the relation between human and land resources. (See Table 1.4.) By this measure, some seemingly sparsely settled countries, especially those of the Gulf, are densely populated.

The fundamental constraint on the development of agricultural land is the result of the climate. The desert cuts a broad swath across the area, from the Atlantic Coast of Morocco to the Arabian Gulf. Except for narrow strips of Mediterranean climate found along the shores of the Maghreb and Turkey and in the Fertile Crescent, most of the remaining land is composed of arid steppe. * With the exception of rare opportunities afforded by perennial rivers, agriculture in the extremely arid interior regions depends on groundwater supplies. The random availability of this water gives rise to a pattern of scattered water holes and oases, some of which are capable of supporting agricultural communities.

Given available technology, additional supplies of water will be forthcoming in the long run under increasing cost conditions. For example, in Saudi Arabia, where substantial groundwater resources have been discovered, unit costs rise sharply as less accessible sources of water are utilized. Water pumped from shallow wells and bore holes is as much as twice as expensive as water from flowing wells, while water pumped from deep wells is three times as expensive.[2] The cost of water from deep wells in the 1960s was equal to the $1.13 per 1,000 gallons assumed for the Jiddah desalting plant. The nominal costs of producing water have been rising steadily. Assuming $80 a ton as the opportunity cost of the energy input in the

---

*Along the Mediterranean coast, average annual rainfall is as high as 20 to 30 inches. In the interior, rainfall is sporadic and light; and in the Sahara and the Arabian deserts, rainfall is nil.

TABLE 1.4

Land Use and the Value of Agricultural Production, Middle Eastern Countries, Mid-1970s
(1975 U.S. dollars)

| Country | Total Area (square kilometers) | Agricultural Area | | | | Population per Square Kilometer of Arable and Cropped Land | Agricultural Value Added per Capita | Agricultural Value Added per Worker | Value Added per Square Kilometer of Agricultural Land |
		Percentage Arable and Permanently Cropped Land	Percentage Meadowland and Pastureland	Percentage Forest Land	Percentage Desert and Other Land				
Major oil states									
Algeria	2,381,730	2.9	15.7	1.0	80.4	220	43	409	1,370
Iran	1,647,991	9.8	6.7	10.9	72.6	205	108	847	7,665
Iraq	434,919	11.5	0.1	4.3	84.1	215	104	639	15,692
Kuwait	17,819	0.1	7.5	0.3	92.3	51,667	—	—	—
Libya	1,759,532	1.4	4.0	0.3	94.3	91	88	1,390	1,880
Oman	217,639	0.2	4.7	0.0	95.1	1,765	—	—	—
Qatar	22,010	0.1	2.3	0.0	97.6	8,636	—	—	—
Saudi Arabia	2,149,680	0.4	39.5	0.7	59.4	630	59	731	358
United Arab Emirates	83,600	0.2	2.4	0.0	97.4	2,036	—	—	—
Other states									
Bahrain	619	2.6	6.5	0.0	90.9	15,625	—	—	—
Egypt	1,001,445	2.8	0.0	0.0	97.2	1,296	73	598	91,348
Israel	20,699	20.1	39.5	5.5	34.9	793	138	4,531	32,936
Jordan	97,738	13.3	1.0	1.3	84.4	202	40	604	6,688
Lebanon	10,399	33.2	1.0	9.1	56.7	889	89	1,739	59,127
Morocco	446,548	16.7	28.0	11.6	43.7	218	57	441	3,627
Northern Yemen	195,000	6.2	35.9	2.0	55.9	529	—	—	—
Southern Yemen	287,678	0.9	31.5	9.0	58.6	630	—	—	—
Sudan	2,505,798	2.8	9.6	36.5	51.1	250	44	159	609
Syria	185,409	31.7	35.0	2.6	30.7	122	60	462	3,237
Tunisia	163,610	27.6	19.9	4.2	48.3	125	75	486	4,829
Turkey	780,576	36.1	33.5	23.4	7.0	138	124	450	6,454

Note: The conversion of agriculture's contribution to local currency 1973 gross domestic product at factor cost to U.S. dollars was made at average exchange rates for the year.

Sources: Food and Agricultural Organization of the United Nations, Production Yearbook, 1974 (Rome: FAO, 1975); and International Bank for Reconstruction and Development, World Tables, 1975 (Washington, D.C.: IBRD, 1976).

mid 1970s, the cost of desalting seawater by flash evaporation, by dis-
tillation, or by vapor compression was $3.75 to $4.00 per 1,000 gal-
lons. [3] Without rigorously economizing on the use of water, agriculture through irrigation will not be worth its cost in desert climates.
Clearly, the lack of water imposes a serious constraint on agricultural
development.

Although water is a necessary factor, it may be difficult to expand the area of cultivation, even when additional water resources
are available. Because of the widespread arid conditions, good soils
with high organic content are in short supply. In general, proportional
increases in water, land, and the other agricultural factors of production are hard to contrive. Even in areas served by major river
systems, such as the Tigris-Euphrates and the Nile, the lack of good
soils is a serious constraint on the expansion of cultivation.

The Tigris-Euphrates has been utilized for irrigation purposes
for over 7,000 years. Although the mineral content of both streams
is moderate, the drainage quality of the Mesopotamian Plain is poor.
Through the millenia, flooding has been followed by evaporation and
transpiration of plants, leaving a residue of salt in the soils. South
of Baghdad, some soils have become so salty that no crops can be
grown, and, elsewhere, only salt-tolerant barley can be grown (at
low yield). The problem can be gauged by observing that in 2400 B.C.,
wheat yields of 2,000 kilograms per hectare were recorded, along
with concern for increasing salinity. [4] In 1972-74, average Iraqi
wheat yields were 1,060 kilograms per hectare. (See Table 1.5.) At
the present time, wheat is grown mostly on rain-watered land because
of the high salt content of the irrigated fields.

In contrast to Iraqi conditions, the Nile Valley benefited from the
flushing action of summer floods, which drained back into the channel
as the river subsided. The regularity of August flooding, the good
drainage, which prevented harmful salt accumulation, and the high
sediment content of the flood waters, which maintained fertility, accounted for excellent natural conditions for primitive agriculture.

Today, the situation has changed, and a new managerial regimen is required. The High Dam precludes the flooding of the Nile
Valley, and, henceforth, sediment will accumulate in Lake Nasser.
The planners expect the new dam to make available through regulated
usage an extra 6.1 million acre-feet of water for irrigation. Although
this represents a gain of approximately 16 percent of the volume previously available and could facilitate the irrigation of about 1 million
acres of additional land above Lake Nasser, Egypt has only about
850,000 unutilized acres of soil both suitable for crops and accessible
to the new water. [5] It appears that good land rather than water has
become the relatively scarce factor. Furthermore, the spread of
perennial irrigation, augmented by the dam, can be expected to con-

TABLE 1.5

Representative Yields in Agriculture, Middle Eastern Countries, Japan, and the United States

Average Annual Yields
(100 kilograms per hectare)

Country	Wheat		Barley		Maize		Cotton (lint)	
	1948-52	1972-74	1948-52	1972-74	1948-52	1972-74	1948-52	1968-71
Major oil states								
Algeria	6.2	5.9	6.9	7.9	9.1	10.0	1.9	2.0
Iran	9.0	8.8	10.1	6.8	10.6	9.9	2.0	4.8
Iraq	4.8	10.6	7.7	11.6	6.8	17.8	1.4	2.5
Kuwait	–	–	–	18.7	–	41.1	–	–
Libya	0.9	4.8	2.4	5.9	8.2	8.7	–	–
Saudi Arabia	13.7	12.5	8.9	15.6	–	54.0	–	–
Other states								
Egypt	18.4	33.5	19.2	28.1	20.9	37.3	5.2	7.6
Israel	6.6	25.1	8.6	12.3	10.3	58.8	–	11.2
Jordan	7.0	8.0	8.3	4.8	–	8.3	–	–
Lebanon	7.3	11.9	12.3	9.5	18.9	9.2	3.3	3.7
Morocco	6.1	9.4	7.3	10.2	5.8	7.1	2.5	3.8
Northern Yemen	10.4	10.9	12.5	12.1	12.0	15.9	5.2	3.4
Southern Yemen	16.4	10.5	16.7	27.8	–	–	4.5	4.4
Sudan	11.8	13.5	7.5	10.6	10.0	7.5	3.6	5.4
Syria	7.7	9.3	8.7	7.5	13.2	13.6	2.8	–
Tunisia	4.9	7.6	3.7	6.7	12.5	17.2	–	–
Turkey	10.0	12.7	11.5	13.3	12.5	17.2	2.5	6.9
Japan	18.5	26.6	20.5	27.7	14.3	17.5	–	–
United States	11.2	20.6	14.3	21.7	24.9	54.3	3.2	5.1

Source: Food and Agricultural Organization of the United Nations, Production Yearbook (Rome: FAO), various issues.

tribute to the problem of water-logged land. With the loss of the natural flushing action of the Nile, salt accumulation will become an increasing problem. Therefore, both Iraq and Egypt have need of improved drainage facilities, although for different reasons.

Most of the countries, lacking water resources comparable to the Nile or the rivers of Iraq, are poor in terms of land that is suitable for agricultural production. (See Table 1.4.) Urban and desert land account for most of the area, and forest lands are scarce. Range and meadowlands are more extensive, although their quality undoubtedly varies widely, from scattered thorn bushes to grassland. The hazards of rapid population growth are clear when considered in relation to these unpromising agricultural conditions.

The populations of the nonoil countries, in particular, continue to rely on agriculture as a prime source of income. If the population of the representative country grows at 3 percent a year, it will double in 24 years. Under prevailing conditions, it will be extraordinarily difficult to maintain the expansion of agricultural output at a corresponding rate. Unless productivity can be increased by steadily improving technology and substituting other factors for marginal land, domestic agriculture will become progressively insufficient.

Although production for the market is increasing, much effort is still devoted to the subsistence of the farmer and his family. Typically, methods of cultivation are primitive: traditional wooden plows and hand tools are still in use. Consequently, the yields of major crops per hectare are relatively low. In the mid-1970s, per capita agricultural value added was less than $100 in most of the countries. (See Table 1.4.) Even where man/land ratios are relatively favorable, the use of machinery is not particularly advanced nor is the use of such productive factors as commercial fertilizers and insecticides. (See Table 1.6.) The Middle East's factor-proportions problem is reflected in value added per worker in agriculture. (See Table 1.4.) Only in Israel was value added per worker high in terms of world standards in the mid-1970s. Elsewhere in the area, value added per worker was mostly from $400 to $800.

Egypt and Israel provide an instructive illustration of the wide variation in factor combinations possible in agricultural production. While the agricultural systems of both countries are effectively organized, they represent the choices of very different techniques. Israel's technology is capital intensive, while Egypt's is highly labor intensive.

In the overpopulated Nile Valley, there are relatively few sources of employment outside of agriculture, whereas Israel's alternative employment situation is much more favorable. Consequently, Egypt employs over six times as many workers per square kilometer of

TABLE 1.6

Factor Proportions in Agriculture, Middle Eastern Countries, 1973

| Country | Percent Irrigated | Resources Relative to Arable Land and Land under Permanent Crops | | | |
		Agricultural Workers per Square Kilometer	Tractors per Square Kilometer	Metric Tons of Nitrogen Fertilizer per Square Kilometer	Metric Tons of Phosphate Fertilizer per Square Kilometer
Major oil states					
Algeria	4	23	0.46	1.39	1.24
Iran	33	25	0.15	1.08	0.69
Iraq	74	34	0.19	0.50	0.31
Libya	5	5	0.15	0.27	0.23
Saudi Arabia	20	49	0.12	0.46	0.15
Other states					
Egypt	100	153	0.66	13.32	2.63
Israel	42	24	4.25	7.25	3.59
Jordan	5	13	0.27	0.08	0.04
Lebanon	20	44	0.89	11.20	6.87
Morocco	11	28	0.19	0.89	0.62
Sudan	20	66	0.12	0.97	—
Syria	11	15	0.19	0.58	0.12
Tunisia	2	19	0.46	0.42	0.39
Turkey	7	37	0.54	1.51	1.00

Source: Food and Agricultural Organization of the United Nations, Production Yearbook, 1974 (Rome: FAO, 1975).

arable and cropped land as does Israel. On the other hand, Israel uses over six times as many tractors per square kilometer of farm-land as does Egypt. These differences in factor proportions are re-flected in value added per agricultural worker. Israel's per worker value added in the mid-1970s was eight times greater than Egypt's.

Considerable variations are apparent in the application of other factors of production. Israel, for example, uses nearly twice the amount of insecticides and other pest killers per unit of land as Egypt. Differences in fertilizer usage also support the impression of dis-tinctly different agricultural regimens. Reflecting differences in the quality of soils and growing conditions, Egypt's use of nitrogen is about twice that of Israel's, but Israel uses somewhat more phosphate per unit of land. (See Table 1.6.)

In spite of the very different techniques of production these dis-parate proportions imply, both regimens are productive in terms of physical yields per unit of land. (See Table 1.5.) In addition, the average yields of both countries have been rising over the long run. Although controls have provided some misallocation, these distinctly different agricultures still represent exemplary uses of available resources.

Unfortunately, the evidence suggests that production is less well organized elsewhere in the area. Development efforts in most Middle Eastern countries are focused on industrialization, even though about half of the people ultimately depend on agriculture for income. In the states lacking great mineral wealth, rapid population growth means that renewed emphasis will have to be accorded agricultural develop-ment.

PETROLEUM RESOURCES

The Middle East holds substantial quantities of natural wealth in forms other than oil reserves—for example, the phosphate deposits of the Maghreb, which contain nearly half of the world's known reserves of that mineral.* In the area at large, extensive mineral surveying has taken place in the past decade, as firms and governments have searched for new sources of prosperity and for the means to greater economic diversification. Despite these efforts, petroleum remains of such overwhelming economic and geopolitical importance that other mineral resources are relatively insignificant.

---

*Oil, potash, phosphates, and potassium compounds are the major natural assets of commercial importance.

The development of the Middle Eastern oil industry began in 1901 with the granting of a concession by the Persian government to William Knox D'Arcy, a British engineer. In exchange for the rights to search for and exploit petroleum resources in Persia, excluding the northern provinces where Russian influence was strong, the terms of the concession required the operating company or companies to pay the Persian government £20,000 in cash and £20,000 in stock. In addition, the Persian government was to receive 16 percent of annual net profits, plus a small annual payment of about £4,000.[6]

The British government took an interest in the search for oil from the beginning. At that time, it was determined to convert the Royal Navy from coal to oil, but the British Empire lacked a secure and adequate source of petroleum. In 1907, Great Britain reached an agreement with Russia whereby the latter was awarded a zone of influence in northern Persia and Great Britain was recognized as the dominant foreign power in the south. A neutral zone was left in the center. The Admiralty arranged for financial support of D'Arcy's search activities, and oil was struck in 1902. In 1909, the Anglo-Persian Oil Company (APOC) was formed, and a refinery was built in the Gulf on the island of Abadan. In 1914, the British government moved to acquire 51 percent of the APOC stock (outstanding). These events established the precedents of petroleum exploitation through concessions granted by host countries to foreign enterprise, equity participation and profit sharing by host countries, and the participation by the concessionaire's home government in Middle Eastern enterprise.

During the interwar years, oil operations spread around the northern end of the Gulf into Iraq, Kuwait, and Saudi Arabia. In this period, the industry was controlled by the major international companies, often referred to as the "seven sisters."* After World War II, new discoveries opened the way to operations in North Africa. Recent years have produced significant changes in the composition of the industry, pricing policies, and roles of the host governments. These are discussed at length in Chapter 5.

Table 1.7 provides some measure of the size and distribution of Middle Eastern petroleum resources. In 1976, the area contained 363 billion barrels of published proved oil reserves, which, at that time, represented 61 percent of the world's total. The distribution of these reserves is uneven in relation to population, as Saudi Arabia,

---

*These were the Standard Oil Company of New Jersey (Exxon), Royal-Dutch/Shell, British Petroleum Company (BP), Gulf Oil Corporation, Texas Company (Texaco), Standard Oil Company of California, and Socony Mobil Oil Company.

TABLE 1.7

Crude Oil Production and Reserves, Middle Eastern Countries, 1976

Country	Year of Discovery	Cumulative Production (millions of barrels)	1976 Production (millions of barrels)	Proved Reserves (millions of barrels)	Reserves/Production Ratio	Reserves/Cumulative Production Ratio
Algeria	1956	4,143.2	392.40	6,800.0	17	1.60
Bahrain	1932	601.0	21.20	290.0	14	0.50
Egypt	1938	1,484.6	118.60	1,950.0	16	1.30
Iran	1908	23,275.0	2,160.80	63,000.0	29	2.70
Iraq	1909	11,200.0	832.20	34,000.0	41	3.00
Israel	1955	15.2	0.30	1.2	4	0.10
Kuwait	1938	17,257.1	711.80	67,400.0	95	3.90
Libya	1959	9,783.7	704.50	25,500.0	36	2.60
Morocco	1947	15.3	0.04	0.2	5	0.01
Neutral Zone	1953	2,569.6	169.70	6,300.0	37	2.50
Oman	1963	967.1	133.20	5,800.0	44	6.00
Qatar	1940	2,410.4	177.00	5,700.0	32	2.40
Saudi Arabia	1938	25,882.6	3,111.60	110,000.0	35	4.30
Syria	1956	300.0	63.90	2,200.0	34	7.30
Tunisia	1964	279.9	28.10	2,700.0	96	9.70
Turkey	1940	283.6	24.50	390.0	16	1.40
United Arab Emirates	1958	3,532.2	709.90	31,200.0	44	8.80
Area total		104,000.5	9,359.70	363,231.4	39	3.50
Area as percent of world		—	43.10	60.6		

Sources: "Worldwide Report," Oil and Gas Journal 74, no. 52 (December 27, 1976): 104-43; and BP Statistical Review of the World Oil Industry, 1976 (London: British Petroleum Company, 1977), pp. 18-19.

the United Arab Emirates, and Kuwait have large per capita holdings, but per capita reserves are relatively modest or nonexistent elsewhere.

By 1976, more than 104 billion barrels of crude oil had been lifted in the area since the inception of the modern industry. The enormity of Middle Eastern reserves can be gauged from the estimation that more than three times this amount remained to be lifted. At the 1976 annual rate of production of 9 billion barrels, the Middle Eastern proved reserves/output ratio shows that production could last another 39 years.

Although it is a commonly used indication of production potential, the proved reserves/output ratio is not an accurate indicator of how long oil production actually will continue. For one thing, prospective or probable reserves are not included in the numerator, and new additions will continue to be made in the proved reserves category for years to come. Furthermore, variations in worldwide economic activity cause shifts in demand and current output. A short-term decline in output can cause a temporary rise in the reserves/output ratio, as happened in 1975. Other things being the same, the assessment of reserve life made during a recession year could give a different impression from one made during a boom year. Finally, states sometimes revise their reported proved reserves because of research findings or for political reasons. Saudi Arabia, for example, abruptly cut its estimated reserves for January 1976 from 148.6 billion barrels to 107.8 billion barrels only to restore the estimate to 151.4 billion barrels in 1977. This resulted in substantial variations in the reserves/output ratio for the whole Middle East. For these reasons, the reserves/production ratio should not be used in forecasting without suitable qualifications.

Although the ultimate size of reserves and the duration of production in the Middle East are imponderables, there is greater certainty now about relative costs of production. The incremental unit cost of Middle Eastern crude, including finding, developing, and operating costs, are the lowest in the world. In the 1980s, per barrel necessary costs in 1972 dollars are expected to range from 15¢ to 20¢ on the Arabian Gulf. In contrast, North Sea oil is expected to cost $1.50 to $2.00 per barrel, and in the United States, medium-cost oil is forecast at $3.30 to $6.70 per barrel.[7] Since per barrel prices for Gulf oil have risen to 60 to 80 times operating costs, economic profits at the lifting stage of the production process are exceptionally large for oil from this source.

Oil reserves are providing the exporting countries with levels of income far in excess of those that otherwise would have been achieved. Petroleum resources thus are serving to compensate for deficiencies in agricultural resources and human skills. The relationship among resources, income growth, and economic development is complex, however, so that, in certain cases, growth based on the exploitation of natural resources can occur without commensurate economic development.

WEALTH AND DEVELOPMENT

It is customarily assumed in economic discussions that more goods and services are better than fewer goods and services. Increasing per capita income in a society is taken to mean betterment in the sense of material well-being. On a cross-country basis, those societies having higher average incomes are assumed to be better off than those in which average incomes are lower, and citizens of the higher-income countries are assumed to enjoy a wider range of choice and opportunity. In the world at large, this is an acceptable measure of welfare, but it should be viewed with skepticism in relation to the contemporary Middle East.

The main difficulty involved in drawing welfare conclusions from per capita income figures for the Middle East is that they fail to take into account differences among countries in the distribution of income. Income inequality is particularly large among the major oil exporters. Although rapid growth of output and the recent sharp rise in unit prices have led to skyrocketing average per capita incomes, there tends to be a substantial time lag between the government's receipt of oil revenue and improvement in the real welfare of ordinary people.* As the world's greatest oil reserves happen to have been found among the more traditional and least-developed countries of the Middle East, per capita income will be only loosely related to real development and social welfare in the region for at least a generation.

Compared with the developed industrial countries, per capita gross national product (GNP) generally has been low in the Muslim Middle East, but with the sixfold rise in posted oil prices between 1971 and 1974, this relationship was drastically changed. Per capita

---

*This lag is implied in the term rentier state, which was applied to Middle Eastern oil-exporting countries by H. Mahdavy to suggest that there is a loose connection at best between their domestic economic systems and the oil rents received by their governments. See H. Mahdavy, "The Patterns and Problems of Economic Development in Rentier States: The Case of Iran," in Studies in the Economic History of the Middle East, ed. M. A. Cook (London: Oxford University Press, 1970), pp. 428-29.

incomes in the United Arab Emirates and Kuwait are now the highest in the world, and, assuming the continuation of high oil prices, per capita GNP in Libya and much of the Arabian peninsula may soon exceed those of the industrial world.

Among the Muslim countries of the Middle East, a significant relationship exists between income and oil wealth. (See Table 1.3.) Per capita incomes tend to vary with per capita oil reserves. Statistical evidence suggests that the linear relationship between per capita oil wealth and per capita income explains 94 percent of the cross-country variation in per capita income.* Although the relative size of the professional class is also positively related to income, it is of far less significance. Other forms of wealth, such as human capital and supplies of arable land, contribute little to explaining cross-country variation in per capita income.

Oil compensates for the absence of indigenous factors normally associated with growth and development. Until the recent nationalizations of foreign enterprise, government oil receipts were essentially a rental income stream that bore little or no connection to indigenous thought or effort. Although foreign enterprise generated some domestic skills and the development of oil enclaves entailed the growth of related professional services, oil revenues flowed in with little reference to domestic resources other than petroleum.

Ordinarily, economic growth is associated with improvements in the quality of life of the bulk of the population, but this relationship is not always confirmed in the Middle East. The idiosyncracies of oil-derived change mean that income growth need not imply develop-

---

*The quality of the relationship between per capita income (y) and various forms of wealth (x) in Muslim countries is indicated by the following coefficients of determination (r^2):

x	r^2
Oil reserves per capita	0.9399
Arable land per capita	0.1339
Literacy rate	0.0040
Professional rate	0.2586

The close linear dependence between oil and income does not, of course, prove causality. But it does mean that, when oil holdings are larger in relation to the population, income will tend to be larger also and that oil reserves are an excellent predictor of income.

ment. Since oil revenue can grow with little reference to domestic factors other than oil reserves, the stimuli for development that expanding sectors normally provide the general economy may be weak. Social and economic development have tended to lag behind income growth in the oil states.

A comparison of per capita incomes with selected indicators serves to reveal some of the paradoxes of Middle Eastern development. In the more affluent oil states, such as Kuwait, Libya, and Saudi Arabia, the defining of petroleum value added as industrial output has raised that sector's product share to high levels, both in relation to the rest of the Middle East and to the Third World in general. * Furthermore, oil production has raised industry's share in the labor force far above what it otherwise would be in the major petroleum states. Even so, industrial shares in product and the labor force are not always reliable indicators of real economic development in the Middle East. Nonoil countries may succeed in promoting a more broadly based industrial expansion than that found in the oil states, even though the latter's industrial share in the value of production may be statistically larger. As an illustration, Egypt has a much more developed industrial base than do most of the petroleum-exporting countries. Although industrial shares in labor and product are enlarged in the long run by the presence of substantial oil reserves, the industrialization produced has been of a narrow, single-product type, and much of the work has been done by expatriate labor. This kind of development is usually not reflected in other indicators of general progress.

UN studies suggest that the level of fertility, as measured by the gross reproduction rate (GRR), † is a reliable indicator of economic and social development. International research shows that GRRs of over 2.0 are closely associated with low levels of development. ‡

---

*The industrial sector is defined as including mining, manufacturing, electric power, gas and water, construction, transportation, and communication activities.

†The GRR is defined as

the average number of daughters that would be born per woman in a group of women, all surviving, to the end of the potentially reproductive period of life and bearing daughters at each age in accordance with the rates prevailing among women of various ages in the area and during the period under consideration (United Nations, Population Bulletin of the United Nations, no. 7 [1963], p. 10).

‡GRRs in excess of 2.0 have been found to be associated with low per capita consumption, subsistence agriculture, low literacy

In terms of GRR, the evidence suggests a lower level of development in the major oil states than in Lebanon, Turkey, and Israel, countries without substantial oil holdings. In the area at large, the relationship between per capita income and fertility is random.* Like fertility, life expectancy tends to undergo a significant change as a society progresses. In Western Europe, the dramatic rise in life expectancy from 47 to 67 years in the first half of the twentieth century reflects this. At present, European life expectancy is nearly 71 years. In the Middle East, only in Israel and Kuwait does life expectancy fall in or near the range associated with modern development. As noted earlier, life expectancy is about 55 years in most of the area, and it is substantially lower in the Yemen, the Sudan, and Saudi Arabia. On a cross-country basis, the relationship between per capita income and life expectancy is not particularly close.†

In conclusion, it is evident that, in the Middle East, great wealth in the form of mineral resources need not be associated with an advanced state of economic development, nor do relatively high per capita incomes necessarily imply a high degree of social welfare. The data show that some of the major oil states may be among the least advanced in terms of balanced modern development. If modern development is to be achieved, this great resource wealth must be used judiciously to redress imbalances among the other factors of production.

NOTES

1. For a useful survey of Middle Eastern culture, including the extended family, see Raphael Patai, "The Middle East as a Cultural Area," Middle East Journal 6 (1952): 1-21.

2. David J. Burdon and Galip Otkun, Hydrological Control of Development in Saudi Arabia, Twenty-third International Geological Congress, vol. 12 (Prague, 1968), p. 152.

3. "Water Resources: Growing Shortages and Some Middle East Solutions," Middle East Economic Digest (special report on water), April 29, 1977, p. 12.

4. M. Clawson, H. H. Landsberg, and L. T. Alexander, The Agricultural Potential of the Middle East (New York: American Elsevier, 1971), p. 117.

rates, and an absence of educational and health facilities, mass communications, and public information services. It is thus a useful measure of the general state of economic and social development.

*The coefficient of determination is only 0.0044.

†The coefficient of determination is 0.2075.

5. Ibid., p. 28.

6. Geroge W. Stocking, Middle East Oil (Nashville, Tenn.: Vanderbilt University Press, 1970), p. 10.

7. Organization for Economic Cooperation and Development, Energy Prospects to 1985, vol. 2 (Paris: OECD, 1974), p. 95.

2

CHANGE AND CONTINUITY
IN THE MIDDLE EAST

Economic development is a gradual process, and, as the economy changes, so must institutions evolve to meet changing needs. Significant institutional changes have occurred in the Middle East, but, along with change, there has been a vital thread of continuity provided by the law of Islam and the traditional market system. These institutions have survived foreign conquest and economic decay; they continue to fashion behavior and values, even in those modern states that have been most radically restructured.

THE TRADITIONAL MARKET

In the contemporary Middle East, expanding primary export sectors have stimulated the growth of modern ancillary services in the areas of transportation, material processing, and finance but have left other sectors virtually unaffected. The resulting unevenness in the general development is implied by the concept of economic dualism in which modern, technologically advanced sectors function in otherwise traditional economies. Dualism is particularly evident in the petroleum-exporting countries, where modern capital-intensive, petroleum-processing sectors flourish alongside traditional sectors, which tend to evolve at much slower rates. As exchange is at the heart of economic life, dual systems afford an opportunity to compare simultaneously two very different price and output conventions.

Modern sector firms make price and output decisions in a manner similar to that followed by monopolistic competitors in the West. In the Middle East, representative modern sector firms are relatively large production or marketing enterprises, often managed by Western-

educated people, selling imported goods or producing under foreign
license. They produce differentiated products or services and can be
assumed to take their rival's pricing and output policies into account
when determining their own. Where there are no modern rivals, they
can be treated as local monopolists. Although firms may follow somewhat differentiated pricing policies, it is plausible to assume that
they know their accounting costs and that their prices are set to cover
average unit cost, plus a profit markup. This done, it is left to the
patronage to determine market clearing output at various "cost-plus"
prices. This price and output convention is in sharp contrast with
procedures found in the suq ("bazaar"), the focal point of traditional
enterprise.

In the suq, uncertain accounting practices and a high volume
of transactions involving the sale of old or nonstandard goods mean
that the cost of production is very loosely related to value. Under
these circumstances, the most plausible hypothesis concerning market behavior is that sellers simply try to maximize profits by charg-
ing as much as the market will bear. Buyers, on the other hand, try
to maximize their satisfactions in consumption by paying the lowest
price possible. The suq is the natural habitat of economic man.

In the suq, trading is essentially a search for value through bargaining. Buyers pit their knowledge and evaluation of the good in question against those of the sellers. The ultimate exchange price will be
somewhere between the minimum amount of money for which the seller
will offer the good and the buyer's maximum bid; these values provide
a floor and ceiling beyond which the exchange price cannot go. When
more than one person at a time is interested in buying a good, the
bargaining process becomes an auction, the method used for the wholesale marketing of farm produce and raw materials. In such cases,
the realized price will lie somewhere between the two highest prices
potential buyers are willing to pay, as the ultimate buyer will have to
outbid his nearest rival.

In the Middle East, exchange is a game of strategy. A buyer or
a seller may feign indifference to the other's bid or offer at one stage
of negotiation and insult, disgust, or scorn at another. Negotiations
may continue for several days, as the buyer returns with new bids
after having made a "final" bid on some previous round of negotiation.

Since sellers seek to maximize profits by pricing as high as the
market will bear, discrimination among buyers may be extreme. A
seller's initial offer price will probably be much higher for Western-
ers or Japanese than for other foreigners. Migrant labor from the
poorer Arab states ultimately will pay less than will the rich for the
same article. Each unique or highly differentiated article has its own
market at each moment in time. Under these conditions, changing
expectations alter both buyers' and sellers' strategies. In this kind

of market prices fluctuate widely. Today's prices depend on who is buying in the market; tomorrow's prices may be very different.

There are similarities between the pricing process of the suq and that of large, modern organizations dealing bilaterally. Although costs are known and products may be homogeneous, bilateral monopoly price and output are theoretically indeterminate. The terms of trade are set through negotiations. Falling into this category are price and output decision making in crude petroleum. Skill in suq bargaining is probably transferable to bilateral monopoly situations; thus, the Arabs' remarkable success in oil negotiations vis-à-vis Western firms and governments can be explained, at least partially, in terms of their discovery of these similarities. Price negotiations are at the heart of everyday economic life in the Middle East, but they are rarely encountered at the retail level in industrial countries.

In the days of the Arab empire, the market was a collection of local suqs, bound together by a network of caravan trails. Today, the relative importance of the traditional suq is gradually declining as modernization, industrial development, and product standardization proceed. Modern marketing institutions are spreading also in response to government programs and changing world market conditions. The traditional market, however, continues to play an important role in organizing and directing economic activity.

TRADITIONAL ISLAM
AND ECONOMIC DEVELOPMENT

Serious consideration of the forces influencing the pattern of development in the Middle East should take Islamic tradition into account, especially those institutions and values that bear most directly on economic behavior. The allocation of resources is influenced by the presence of religious motives. In order to satisfy the requirements of Islam, resources flow into mosque construction, pilgrimages, and charity. But the economic implications go further. Religion implies ethical standards that influence behavior in varying degrees, so that Islam has an indirect as well as a direct bearing on economic activity.

The main sources of Islamic doctrine are the Koran and the sunna. The Koran is believed to be the literal word of God as revealed to Muhammad; the sunna is the words and practices of Muhammad, which were collected from oral tradition. During the eighth and ninth centuries, lawyers and scholars developed the law of Islam, the shari'a, through precedent and reasoning by analogy from the Koran and the sunna. The law was confirmed by the consensus of the community, as seen by theologians in their role as interpreters of the Koran. In a functioning Islamic system, legal specialists issue opinions on doctrinal and legal problems, while judges administer the law. [1]

Law and religious duty were intertwined, since the shari'a was intended to regulate all aspects of life; in practice, however, the shari'a exerted its influence unevenly. It applied most directly to family relations, inheritance, and the conduct of religious foundations and less directly to penal law, constitutional law, taxation, and the law of war. The law of contracts, which guided much of economic life, represents a blending of the ideal shari'a with worldly custom and practice. [2]

Although there are restrictions designed to prevent speculation, the most profound economic constraint imposed by the shari'a is the prohibition of interest. [3] In Islam, usury means not merely exorbitant interest but any interest at all. The role of interest, however, is crucial to an expanding market economy. It is an indication of the productivity of capital in society, and it provides an incentive for saving, without which private resources would not be available for investment. As the price of capital, interest serves to ration scarce resources. Efficient investment decisions require the comparison of the rate of return expected from a capital asset with the market rate of interest. Therefore, one would expect that prohibition of interest would cripple a market economy and that the establishment of an Islamic regime would preclude economic development. This seems to be the conventional attitude of Western economists. With its constraining and theoretically inflexible law, Islam provides a convenient explanation for traditionalism and stagnation in the Middle East.

Yet, the establishment of Islam did not lead to stagnation initially. In fact, the opposite occurred. Conditions improved under the Umayyad caliphate (661-747), and it was during the Abbasid caliphate (747-1258) that Islamic civilization enjoyed its golden age. It is well known that Arab scholars kept Hellenic science and philosophy alive during medieval times. Literature and art flourished, and works in history and geography reached new levels of sophistication. In the realm of economics, the division and specialization of labor increased, craft industries developed, and wealth increased. The Islamic world formed a huge trade bloc, extending from Spain to China and from Russia to Africa. The surge of development under Islam lifted the area to levels of material prosperity and cultural achievement far above those of contemporary Europe. [4]

This outcome is clearly at odds with the expected results of the constraining rules of Islam. In fact, Islam has never been so inflexible and pervasive in practice as it presumes to be in theory. Just as Judaism and Christianity have adjusted to changing conditions and opportunities, so has Islam. There is a symmetrical relationship between economics and religion: if religion influences economic activity, then, surely, economic conditions influence the practice of religion. Muslim entrepreneurs took advantage of the exceptional opportunities for profits that existed in the wake of expanded markets and political unification.

In practice, contracts and obligations were influenced by customary law, which showed more flexibility than the shari'a. For example, it allowed the use of bills of exchange beyond the limits set by the shari'a, and this made possible the development of banking enterprise. Formalized legal devices were used as a means to extralegal ends. In this way, interest was paid while observing the letter of the shari'a. One popular device for this purpose was the double sale, in which the borrower would sell the lender an asset for cash and then immediately buy it back for a greater amount, payable at some future date. The difference in the prices was interest. There were hundreds of such devices, covering all aspects of the law of contracts and obligations. [5]

Insights into medieval Islamic business practices and values are provided by the Cairo Geniza documents,* as edited and interpreted by S. D. Goitein. [6] These documents reveal that capital was mobilized and rewarded through partnership arrangements in which certain partners might provide capital in exchange for a share in the profits, although they were excluded from participation in losses. [7] This system compensated for the lack of a fully developed capital market, but it was clearly less efficient. Since partners usually were required to deal with one another face to face, the opportunities for mediation beyond those provided by merchant bankers were limited.

During the tenth through the thirteenth centuries, banking operations flourished. Gold dinars and silver coins served as the monetary base against which bankers issued promissory notes, which circulated and were regarded as cash. [8] In addition, bankers held stock of foreign coins, which they traded for profit after weighing and assaying them. Since weighing and assaying were costly, coins often were exchanged in sealed purses with their exact value shown on the outside. [9] Bankers also collected and paid drafts similar to modern checks, handled bills of exchange, and made customer loans, usually at an implicit rather than an explicit rate of interest. [10] Bankers invested frequently as partners in an enterprise. [11]

---

*The Cairo Geniza is a unique depository of letters, court records, and accounts of merchants, covering business transactions all over the Islamic Mediterranean world. They provide an excellent picture of Islamic commerce during the tenth through the thirteenth centuries.

Pious Muslims, then as now, must have declined receipt of interest, so that the supply of loanable funds can be assumed to have been reduced below its potential. On the other hand, this dampening effect on development was probably more than offset by the traditional enthusiasm for profits. Trade is considered favorably by the shari'a, and profits appear to have been recognized as the appropriate reward for organizing production and bearing risk. "Profit follows responsibility" is a lawyer's adage from the early days of Islam. [12] In the days of the Cairo Geniza, profits of 13 percent of gross sales appear to have been normal, although some undertakings produced much higher ratios. [13] Ordinary business principles in medieval Islam reveal a fundamental urge to maximize returns from scarce capital.

Ideally, one's money should never be left idle but should be invested in many limited ventures in order to spread the risk. [14] This principle helps explain the failure of capital-intensive enterprise to develop during the period. The ordinary hazards of life, piracy, and military uncertainties made the spreading of risk a prudent policy and the aggregation of large stocks of capital in a single endeavor unlikely.

The economic development that took place under Islam does not constitute an industrial revolution in the nineteenth-century sense, but it is an impressive case of capitalist development within the confines of medieval science and technology. The difference between Islamic development and modern industrialism is largely a matter of scale and technology. Enterprise and ingenuity were effectively guided by the market system during the classic period, and history shows that, when profit opportunities are available, Muslims are capable of making the institutional adjustments needed for their realization.

DECLINE AND STAGNATION OF THE OLD ORDER

It is probable that economic conditions in the eastern wing of the Islamic empire began to decline as early as the tenth century. At that time, the rising costs of the court and bureaucracy began to be met by tax farming, whereby rights to collect extra taxes were distributed to senior officials in lieu of salary.* Governors, usually generals, became autonomous chieftans, who governed through military force.

---

*In the classic Islamic period, taxes were not a deterrent to enterprise. The main tax was the zakat, a 2.5 percent per annum tax on money, cattle, corn, fruit, and merchandise.

In the eleventh century, the Seljuk Turks took control of western Asia, ruling in the name of the Abbasid caliphs. Under their administration, the Mesopotamian system of irrigation canals fell into disrepair and agricultural output declined. This retrogression was exacerbated by waves of Crusader and Mongol invasions, which served to drain off resources in waste and pillage. Trade links to the Orient and northern Europe were severed in the thirteenth century, as Mongol invaders razed Baghdad and ended the Abbasid caliphate.

In the fifteenth century, the Ottoman Turks established a new empire on the wreckage of the Byzantine and Arab empires. This new state brought order and stability to a region spreading from Anatolia to northern Africa, thus giving it control of the trade routes from Europe across the Middle East to Asia. The conditions were right for a renewal of the area's economic development and cultural advance. Political instability had been eliminated, the area was at least temporarily secure from foreign invasion, and the opportunities provided by a strategic location in world trade had been restored. Permanent prosperity, however, proved to be elusive.

Agriculture was the basis of the Ottoman state organization. The welfare of the ordinary people depended on agriculture, public finance relied heavily on land taxes, and the traditional military organization was built around a particular system of property rights.

Beginning as a Turkish emirate on the frontier of Byzantium, the early Ottoman state was not extensively monetized; land taxes were collected in kind. As the state expanded, conquered lands were distributed to cavalrymen, who administered them and retained a share of the taxes as salary. In this way, the provincial armies were maintained and the military was provided with a vested interest in agricultural productivity. Large holdings in the hands of the military effectively precluded the rise of strong local aristocracies and thus served to maintain centralized power, a major Ottoman political objective. Small holdings were left to the peasants. Although the Ottoman system provided the peasants with order and security, they could not leave the land without paying compensation to the landlord; thus, the peasant was effectively bound to the land. [15]

The conquest of Egypt in 1517 provided the empire with especially valuable agricultural resources. Although Egyptian agriculture output fell just after the conquest, by the end of the sixteenth century, the irrigation system was fully restored and the cultivated area had been extended. [16] Egypt served as the granary of the empire and provided growing land tax contributions to the treasury until the 1780s. [17]

The formation of new wealth under Ottoman rule is implied by the increasing opulence of Istanbul, the capital and seat of the caliphate, as well as by the growth of other commercial cities—for example, Bursa, which grew wealthy as a center for the international silk trade. As early as 1502, it had more than 1,000 looms in operation and a large and prosperous bourgeoisie. [18]

These indications of increasing prosperity notwithstanding, after the 1590s, the Ottoman state began a long decline into economic stagnation and social decay. Although Ottoman institutions were flawed, the ultimate causes of this retrogression are to be found in events that occurred outside the empire. These were the discoveries of America and the Cape of Good Hope in the late fifteenth century by the more rapidly developing European powers.

By the discovery of passage to the East around the Cape of Good Hope, Europe succeeded in outflanking the Ottoman-controlled Middle East, and, as a consequence, during the sixteenth century the area's involvement in international trade gradually declined. [19] Reinforcing this effect was the Ottoman economic policy of imperial self-sufficiency, while the extension of European markets to America and the Far East, together with rapid technological change, was creating economies of scale, new products, and enlarged profit opportunities for the West. These developments, combined with the European mercantilist policies of import substitution and the favorable balance of trade, meant declining European demand for finished goods of the Ottoman craft industry and the increasing availability of cheaper and more attractive European goods. Ottoman export trade in the sixteenth century tended to become increasingly limited to primary products. The experience of Bursa provides a case in point. In the first half of the sixteenth century, the looms of Bursa produced a large volume of silk cloth for European export. In the latter half of the century, the rise of the European silk industry reduced the demand for Bursa cloth, and the city's silk exports to Europe were limited to thread and raw silk. [20] The seventeenth century found the Ottoman Middle East in the backwater of world trade, economically stagnant, and increasingly confined to the production of primary commodities for the rising nations of Europe. This retrogression was augmented by the devastating effects of the sixteenth-century price revolution.

The flow of bullion from the New World to Spain has long been recognized as an important contributing factor in the industrial revolution. [21] As the inflows were monetized, Spanish prices began to rise, increasing profits and demand for imported goods from Europe and the East. The prices of final goods and services in northern Europe rose faster than money wages and other costs, thus inflating profits. Merchants and manufacturers, in responding to these entrepreneurial incentives, used their increasing real returns for technological innovation and for enlarging the capital stock. In this way, the inflow of bullion from America served as a catalytic agent in the rise of industrial capitalism in Europe.

The effects of bullion inflows were remarkably different in the Ottoman Middle East. O. L. Barkan suggests that the failure of Ottoman officials and institutions to adjust constructively to the challenge of inflation initiated the empire's long decline. [22] The rise in European demand for primary products resulted in the bidding of such basic commodities as wheat, copper, and wool away from Ottoman markets. These were strategic items in Ottoman economic policy, and, at this time, their export was legally prohibited. Contraband exports accelerated, with collusion or participation by high officials. The government thus was unable to enforce its own edicts. The resulting increase in the money supply and depletion of commodity reserves led to accelerating inflation, while traditional production functions precluded immediate supply responses to the higher prices.

Furthermore, Ottoman monetary policy made matters worse. In a series of attempts to maintain the state's command over resources, the government resorted to the debasement of the monetary unit. From 1566 to 1618, the silver content of the akces ("asper") was successively reduced, for an overall reduction of 58 percent.[23] These moves served to cheapen Ottoman goods in relation to European silver and thus to stimulate the inflow of silver and the rise of Ottoman prices. The sharpest reduction in the value of the asper during this period occurred in 1585-86, when it was debased by 44 percent. This action was followed by a period of severe inflation, in which such powerful elements as the bureaucracy, the military, and the religious establishment suffered real income losses.

The relative severity of the Ottoman inflation can be gauged by comparing the behavior of living costs in Istanbul with certain European cases of about the same time. (See Table 2.1.) Following the debasement of the asper, prices in Istanbul rose nearly 3.5-fold from 1586 to 1606, whereas in England and Andalusia, inflation rates were substantially less. Of the three, Ottoman inflation was the most severe and concentrated in time. It took 50 to 60 years in Andalusia and England for prices to double and triple, respectively, but in Istanbul, prices more than tripled in just 20 years.

Although it would be facile to claim that these financial troubles caused the decline of the Ottoman empire, it is clear that they did worsen existing negative trends and introduced new problems. One serious repercussion was the decline of the old landholding system in favor of one characterized by larger holdings, absentee owners, and tax farming. European infantry and firearms already were making the traditional fief-holding cavalry army obsolete, and the strength of this landed class was greatly reduced by inflation. As a means for increasing state revenue, their holdings were converted to crown lands and leased to urban tax farmers. In the process of consolidation, peasants were made landless under the new tax regimen, and agricul-

TABLE 2.1

Inflation in the Sixteenth Century: Price Indexes in Andalusia,
England, and Istanbul

Andalusia[a]		England[b]		Istanbul[c]	
Period	Index	Period	Index	Period	Index
1501–10	100.0	1541–50	100.0	1585–86	100.0
1511–20	97.3	1551–60	167.1	1586–87	147.0
1521–30	131.1	1561–70	196.2	1587–88	174.5
1531–40	158.9	1571–82	216.5	1588–89	200.3
1541–50	203.4	1583–92	250.6	1595–96	242.0
		1593–1602	307.6	1596–97	291.6
				1605–06	345.6

[a]Decennial averages of annual index numbers. The index includes commodities used in victualing and outfitting treasure fleets.

[b]Decennial averages of annual index numbers. The index includes 79 commodities.

[c]Annual index numbers. The index includes food and kitchen goods.

Sources: Andalusia—Earl J. Hamilton, American Treasure and the Price Revolution in Spain, 1501-1650 (Cambridge, Mass.: Harvard University Press, 1934), p. 190; England—Earl J. Hamilton, "American Treasure and the Rise of Capitalism (1500-1700)," Economica 9, no. 27 (November 1929): 352; and Istanbul—Omer L. Barkan, "The Price Revolution of the Sixteenth Century: A Turning Point in the Economic History of the Near East," International Journal of Middle East Studies 6, no. 1 (January 1975): 11.

tural productivity declined. Unemployed peasants swelled the urban populations, while the urban military class and the bureaucracy became increasingly corrupt in the struggle for economic survival. Popular uprisings and protests against the established authority were the result.[24]

In contrast to northern Europe, Ottoman windfall profits financed land and commodity speculation. Inflation sparked no technological innovation or industrial expansion. Although the Ottoman state survived until 1923, its economy stagnated after the sixteenth century, and it steadily declined in relation to the expanding West.

These retrograde social conditions reinforced the hand of the backward-looking orthodox theologians and other conservative elements in society. Innovation in all forms was discouraged. Intellectual and artistic endeavors stagnated. The political power of the religious orthodoxy and conservative elements in the military inhibited reform efforts when they were begun in the eighteenth and nineteenth centuries, thus demonstrating the interplay between economics and the practice of religion.

By the nineteenth century, European economic superiority was overwhelming, and the traditional economic structures began to break down, as cheaper Western goods penetrated the markets in rising volume. Penetration was facilitated by the Anglo-Turkish Commercial Convention of 1838, which opened the Ottoman market to new and relatively cheap European manufactured goods, while making Middle Eastern primary products more accessible to European buyers. The economic effects were a remarkable rise in the value of Ottoman trade with the West and significant changes in the structure of production in the Middle East.

The appearance of new European products in Middle Eastern markets stimulated the formation of new tastes and demands. As European products were preferred over local substitutes, the result was the destruction of many branches of domestic industry. In the Istanbul area alone, the number of producing looms declined from 2,750 in the 1830s to 25 in the 1860s. In Bursa, where 1,000 looms once had been in production, only 75 were operating in the 1840s. The once prosperous leather industry virtually disappeared, and, in the 1860s, only about half of the cotton textile factories were in operation. Only a few uniquely Middle Eastern lines of production, such as Damascus arms, carpets, mother-of-pearl goods, jewelry, and apparel, seem to have survived undamaged. [25]

At the same time, the effective European demand for Ottoman primary products increasingly served to monetize the economy and to extend the area of cultivation. The production of such crops as cotton, silk, tobacco, coffee, dates, wheat, and barley was organized on a cash basis, largely for export.

In the second half of the nineteenth century, foreign capital and entrepreneurship moved into the area. The Suez Canal and various port facilities, a rudimentary rail transport system, and municipal services were developed by European capital, either through loans to Middle Eastern governments or through direct investment. The transportation investments were particularly important in bringing the Middle East into the world system and in lowering transportation costs of world commerce. The Suez Canal, built in 1869, provided savings of 4,500 miles, or 24 days of travel, for shipping between London and Bombay.[26] Railroad mileage in Egypt rose from 300 in 1860 to 2,300 in 1910.[27] These developments and others, such as the Berlin-Baghdad rail project, served to tie the Middle East to the European trade network.

Furthermore, European banks were established in the major cities, providing intermediary ties between European lenders and Middle Eastern governments and other borrowers. In 1914, British, French, and German investments in Turkey amounted to $1.1 billion.[28] In Egypt, total foreign indebtedness in 1914 was approximately $1 billion. Although much of the borrowing by the governments in the nineteenth century led to productive capital formation, considerable extravagence and waste were also associated with the rising public debt. The progressive financial overextension of Middle Eastern governments led to Western fiscal tutelage or outright occupation and control. The Ottoman empire was declared bankrupt in 1875 and surrendered its fiscal sovereignty to its European creditors in 1881. Insolvency led to the British occupation of Egypt in 1882 and to French intervention in Tunisia in 1881 and in Morocco in 1912. France had already occupied Algeria in 1830. Under the mandate system after the Turkish defeat in World War I, Great Britain controlled Iraq, Jordan, and Palestine. Lebanon and Syria were placed under French administration. Thus, in the 1920s, the newly formed Turkish republic, Iran, and the expanding Saudi state in Arabia were the only major independent polities in the Middle East.

The penetration and control of the Middle East by the European powers represent a mixture of positive and negative effects from the point of view of the area itself. The area clearly gained from the importation of European capital and technology; from improvements in medicine, education, and administration; and from the extension of the area of cultivation. The increased use of money and the market implies potential gains through the division and specialization of labor and through the facilitation of real savings and investment. On the other hand, costs were involved that extended well beyond the obvious degradation implied by foreign rule. Control by the West meant that the production structures would tend to evolve in ways that were complementary to those of the West. Consequently, development was confined largely to the export sectors, whose products were usually agricultural or mineral—raw materials for Western industry. Although some ancillary development did occur, the destruction of local craft industries was not followed by the development of modern industry. The complementarity between Middle Eastern and Western economic structures was still strikingly apparent in the years between the World wars. (See Table 2.2.) The major Middle Eastern economies of the day were essentially agricultural, while those of the

TABLE 2.2

Sectoral Shares in Production and the Labor Force: Egypt, Turkey, France, and Great Britain, between World Wars (percent)

Area	Sectoral Shares in Net National Product				Sectoral Shares in Labor Force			
	Year	Agriculture[a]	Industry[b]	Services[c]	Year	Agriculture[a]	Industry[b]	Services[c]
Middle East								
Egypt	1937	49	11	40	1937	71	12	17
Turkey	1938	39	21	40	1935	82	10	8
Europe								
France	1938	24	47	29	1936	36	36	28
Great Britain	1924	4	53	43	1931	6	53	41

[a] Agriculture sector also includes forestry, fisheries, and hunting.

[b] Industry sector includes mining and manufacturing, construction, transportation, communications, and public utilities (electricity, gas, and water).

[c] Services sector includes trade, banking, and public and private services.

Sources: Mahmoud A. Anis, "A Study of the National Income of Egypt," L'Egypt Contemporaine 41, nos. 261 and 262 (1950): 684; United Nations, National Income Statistics of Various Countries, 1938–1948 (Lake Success, N.Y.: United Nations, 1950); Simon Kuznets, Economic Growth of Nations (Cambridge, Mass.: Harvard University Press, 1971), p. 144; and United Nations, Statistical Yearbook, 1948.

leading European powers were largely industrial. Complementarity is particularly apparent in the case of the British and Egyptian economies: the agricultural and industrial shares in output and labor of the one are roughly mirror images of the other. With the coming of real autonomy after World War II, one of the major tasks assumed by the new leadership was the achievement of more diversity in the structure of industry and in the pattern of production.

ARAB SOCIALISM

Western domination of the Middle East produced a spiritual and intellectual reaction among the Muslim peoples, which included a questioning and re-examination of fundamental values and institutions. With the achievement of political independence, the peoples of the area began a search for the means to cultural renaissance and economic prosperity. For some, such as the Wahhabis of Arabia and the Muslim Brotherhood in Egypt, the way to salvation lay in purging society of corrupting influences and in returning to the unaltered institutions of early Islam. Others saw the region's best chance for secular progress in the values of Western liberalism. By adopting Western parliamentary democracy and private industrial capitalism, they sought to modernize the Middle East. Finally, there were those who broke cleanly with much of the past and looked for new vitality in the ideas of the European left and national development (through reliance on single-party state socialism).

Politically, Arab socialism combines local nationalism with the goal of Pan-Arabism and avoids conflict with Islam, which is still the most influential ideology in the region. Socialism is often identified with the egalitarianism of Islam, and the shari'a is still the norm against which modern civil law is evaluated.

Relations with the West and the Communist bloc are governed more by pragmatic considerations than by ideological concerns. Arab leaders have shown remarkable ingenuity in separating ideology from commercial needs. Anticapitalist propaganda has gone hand in hand with heavy reliance on Western technology and industrial expertise.

The original socialist doctrine in the Arab world was that of the Ba'th (Resurrection) party in Syria. The party's original appeal was directed toward those who wished to break the economic and political power of the small ruling elite, which was then composed of well-to-do merchants, landowners, and tribal leaders.

The Ba'th program, although cast in a somewhat vague and utopian mold, provides a general prescription for egalitarian social transformation. Among its provisions are state ownership and control of major natural resources, large industries, and the transporta-

tion, communications, and banking systems. Private property rights
in other sectors of the economy are recognized, within the limits of
the national interest. Worker participation in managerial decisions
and profit sharing in industry are approved, and land reform is prescribed to eliminate the exploitation of landless peasants. The state
is expected to regulate internal and external trade to protect the interests of consumers. Economic planning is the means for industrial
development, and plans are to be financed by state banks. The Ba'thist agenda assumes a parliamentary democratic political framework
and aspires to a unified Arab nation, reaching from Morocco to Iraq.*

Through party influence and actual rule since 1963, many of the
Ba'thist goals have been achieved in Syria. By 1971, 75 percent of
industry was state owned. State industry is divided into a chemical
federation, a food and textile federation, and an engineering federation. Decision making is centered in the Ministry of Industry. Transportation, electricity generation facilities, petroleum refining, and
mineral wealth are state owned. Agriculture and trade are mostly
in private hands, but state controls over prices and resource allocation means de facto state control in these sectors also. Through
representation on management committees, labor has had a voice in
decision making since 1963. Land reform and economic planning
were begun in 1958. Although many of the essentials of the Ba'thist
economic program have been implemented, effective parliamentary
democracy is yet to be established.

Economic reform in Egypt appears to be similar to that in Syria.
But while the Ba'thist officers in Syria took power with an economic
agenda in hand, Colonel Nasser and his small Free Officers movement
had no revolutionary party or ideology behind them when they over-
threw the monarchy in July 1952. Nothing remotely resembling the
Ba'th was available to the Egyptian reformers in 1952. They had,
nonetheless, three broad goals in mind: the overthrow of the monarchy, the elimination of foreign influence, and social reform.[29]
The first objective was accomplished in an almost bloodless coup.
The others remain the objects of a continuing quest.

Although the Free Officers took power without strong ideological
commitment or a blueprint for change, their nationalism, their determination to reform society, and the ancient tradition of centralized
authority in Egypt made evolution toward a command economy highly
probable. Economic individualism had come to be identified with
monopoly and colonialism. The tradition of centralized control of the
lives of ordinary people has a long history in the Nile Valley. Exten-

---

*Ba'thism has guided policy in Iraq since 1963.

sive irrigation and flood control systems are essentially public goods, the creation and maintenance of which naturally devolve to the state. Control over collective agricultural enterprise was a key factor in the rise of state power in the ancient Middle East. [30]

The evolution to a bureaucratically controlled economy can be seen as occurring in three phases. The period 1952-56 was one in which reform was undertaken within an essentially free enterprise environment. During the period, the government began the preparatory measures for the Aswan High Dam project and established the Halwan steel and iron plant in joint enterprise with the private sector. At this time, the government was concerned with encouraging private initiative. Business leaders were consulted on policy, strikes were made illegal, and arbitration machinery was established. In this period, the government was working to break the political power of the landlords and to spur industrialization, while still relying on the private sector as the mainspring of development.

By the mid-1950s, Cold War political forces had led to a clear change in the government's economic stance. Through responses to such external challenges as declining cotton sales to the West and the withdrawal of the U.S. offer of aid for building the Aswan Dam, the Nasser government made a series of moves that culminated in the nationalization of the Suez Canal, the sequestration of certain foreign assets, and, finally, the Suez War of 1956. In the process, the government assumed a more authoritarian and interventionist economic policy at home.

The years 1957-60 represent a period of guided capitalism in which the state extended its control of enterprise but stopped short of nationalizing domestic industry. In 1957 all publicly owned industrial and commercial property was put under the control of an agency known as the Economic Organization (1957-61). This agency controlled about one-third of the output of the modern industrial sector and 20 percent of its employment. In 1959, the Ministry of Industry was empowered to regulate the purpose, establishment, expansion, and location of industrial plants. The government already owned shares in Misr group enterprises. Since these dominated Egyptian industry, the government was provided with a device for influencing the pattern of investment. The nationalization of foreign banks and insurance companies, plus exchange controls, gave the government additional means for controlling investment and production. This influence extended into agriculture through the control of agricultural credit. Through the supplying of the credit, the government acquired influence over choices regarding land use, crops, seeds, and fertilizers. The reversal of public and private roles is indicated by the following data: in 1952-53, 72 percent of gross capital formation was undertaken by the private sector; in 1959-60, 74 percent of investment was undertaken by the state. [31]

Although the government continued to pay lip service to socially responsible private enterprise, the initiation of central planning led to the authorities to recognize an inherent conflict between comprehensive planning and private decision making. The government was forced to make fundamental choices concerning the economic system. In 1959, a comprehensive five-year plan was prepared for the period 1960-65. The fundamental ambivalence in the government's attitude toward the private sector is revealed in the planned sources and uses of capital during the first two years of the planning period. For 1960-62, about four-fifths of total investment was to be made by the public sector, yet 70 percent of the required savings was to be provided by the domestic private sector, 20 percent was to come from abroad, and only 10 percent from the public sector. Although the government raised permissible corporate dividend rates from 10 to 20 percent and tried to foster private saving with favorable interest remunerations, the demoralized private sector failed to meet the target. With its plan in jeopardy, the government undertook a new series of nationalization measures.

In 1960, Bank Misr was nationalized completely, and the Misr group enterprises took over the newspapers, the tea trade, and pharmaceuticals. Bank Misr and its companies became known as the Misr Organization, a national-Socialist institution.[32] Stock market values sank, and in June 1961 the Alexandria futures market was closed as the state took over the raw cotton trade. In 1961, all remaining banks were nationalized, as was the Khedival Shipping Line and 44 firms in the timber, cement, electricity, and transport industries. In addition, the state expropriated the capital of 86 commercial and light manufacturing companies. When the bourgeoisie petitioned the army to intervene, the government responded by imprisoning representatives of the old elite and sequestering the property of hundreds of wealthy persons.

In May 1962, President Nasser presented the National Charter, describing the new economic system as a socialist one, in which the public sector would lead in all areas and bear responsibility for fulfilling the development plan. The public sector was described as including the infrastructure, finance, and heavy industry. Mixed ownership was prescribed for the light and medium industries and external trade. Private ownership was restricted to land, small industry, and internal trade. All production was subject to state control and direction. As the "open door" policy of 1973 represented an attempt to liberalize parts of this system and to resuscitate the private sector, it can be said to have marked the ending of the era of expanding statism.

Although Ba'thist ideology must have had some influence on the Nasser government, especially during the period of union with Syria (1958-61), it is clear that Egypt's drift into Arab socialism was the result of responses to a long series of challenges to the regime. It was not a fulfillment of ideological preconceptions, as was the case in Syria.

Although socialism in both Egypt and Syria bears a similarity to classical European and Marxian socialism, there is a distinct difference. European socialism, as it developed in the nineteenth century, was a working-class movement. In Syria and Egypt, it is the ideology and tool of the new middle class—junior officers, teachers, smaller landowners, and civil servants. These formed a relatively small educated class, which stood to gain in power under a new order in which the state would play a more dominant role. The Ba'th is yet to become a mass party; it continues to serve ethnic and regional interests in Syria. In 1962, President Nasser established the Arab Socialist Union, the only legal political party in Egypt until Sadat's experimentation with parliamentary democracy in the later 1970s. The purpose of Nasser's move was to develop leadership and to broaden participation and political support among the middle-income groups. 33 Clearly, socialism in neither Egypt nor Syria thus far rests on the proletarian foundation of the Marxist-Leninist tradition.

In contrast, socialism has deeper roots in Algeria. The movement of labor to and from France and political activity among the French colonialists contributed to the spread of European ideas among the working class. The French and Algerian Communist parties were active among the workers in Algeria in the 1930s, and socialist ideas had been associated with the independence movement since its inception in the 1920s. Until its suppression by the French in 1956, the Communist General Confederation of Labor was the largest labor union in Algeria and included most of organized Algerian labor. Thus, it appears that socialist ideology was more widely understood and accepted in Algeria than in Egypt or Syria when the governments undertook radical socialist transformation.

By virtue of its leadership in the struggle for independence, the National Liberation Front (FLN) won recognition by France as the legitimate representative of the Algerian people. The constitution confirmed the FLN as the legal party of Algeria. At the Tripoli Conference of 1962, and in the constitution, the party declared that a socialist society was its goal. The FLN, however, rejected atheistic communism. (Algerian socialism is a blending of traditional Islam with Marxist ideas. Since Islam is essentially egalitarian, nonritualistic, and philanthropic, with emphasis on group solidarity, the result is an eclectic ideology that blends the common features.)

The economic aspects of the program outlined at Tripoli in 1962 included proposals for the nationalization of banks, transport, foreign trade, and mineral resources. The Tripoli program also proposed land reform in order to reduce large holdings to the benefit of landless

Algerian peasants. Private exchanges of land were to be banned in order to prevent further accumulation by the bourgeoisie.

In practice, the pattern of economic policy after the war for independence has been shaped by the problems created by the large French exodus. The departure of about 1 million Europeans and their liquid assets represented an economic loss that has yet to be fully offset. Entrepreneurs, technicians, skilled workers, teachers, and administrators left the country; factories and farms were abandoned. The government's response was the institution of autogestion, a system of workers' self-management. In this way, the state fell heir to the abandoned French assets, which were to be run by management boards elected by the workers, together with a state-appointed director.

The nationalization of French property brought approximately half of the cultivable area under state control. Since 1971, the government has pursued a policy of redistributing large private holdings and state land not in the self-managed sector to landless peasants (who are organized into cooperatives). Despite these efforts, the performance of Algerian agriculture has been inadequate. The output of major crops has grown little, and the self-managed sector has required subsidization. As a consequence, the bureaucracy has become increasingly involved in agriculture and its problems.

Similarly, public authority dominates the industrial sector. The state either owns or has a controlling interest in heavy industry and is gradually extending its control over light industry and trade as well. Although autogestion is a basic feature of Algeria's socialist ideology, the intrusion of bureaucracy casts doubt on its reality. It may be that Algeria's progress as a command economy precludes the development of effective worker participation in decision making.

Generalizing on these major cases, it appears that Arab socialism is an amalgam of state capitalism, cooperative institutions, the welfare state, private enterprise, and the traditional market system. It thus lies between the mixed capitalist system of the West and the communism of the East. Since the industrial sectors that are controlled directly by the state are still relatively small, it follows that a large part of economic activity is still conducted in traditional ways and through traditional institutions.

Although the Arab socialist economies are probably still in a malleable state, a reversal of the trend can be painful in a poor country; Egypt's experience demonstrates this. At the core of the Egyptian system of control is a complex structure of regulated prices that have little or no connection with opportunity costs. Imported goods are sold in state enterprises at a fraction of their true costs; by the mid-1970s, the subsidies required to maintain these artificial prices had reached $1 billion, or nearly a tenth of the Egyptian GNP. Egypt could no longer afford the system, but when the regime attempted to reduce the subsidies and raise food prices in 1977, the worst riots since the revolution of 1952 ensued, as the great mass of the population was already living close to the margin of subsistence. To squeeze them further could lead to revolution, but the continuation of the present system wastes resources and discourages economic expansion. Once this degree of atrophy has been reached, large-scale and sustained international financial assistance may be the only way to bridge the transition to a more fruitful balance between central authority and individual initiative guided by the market.

SUMMARY AND CONCLUSIONS

The law of Islam and the traditional market system provide the Middle East with two strands of continuity in a world of change. Even in those countries where radical reforms have occurred, the religion and the suq still guide the lives of the great majority.

The surge of commercial energy and material prosperity under early Islam was possible because of the extension of the market in the wake of Arab conquest. As it generated new variations and commercial arrangements, the suq process facilitated trade, growth, and development. The law of Islam, the shari'a, was applied selectively and with discretion, so that inhibiting aspects, such as the prohibition of interest, were not the obstacles to material progress as they may seem to be in the abstract. At the same time, the shari'a was used to provide the basic security of persons and property, without which civilized society cannot endure. This initial prosperity was eroded by external forces. Invasions by Seljuk Turks, Mongols, and Crusaders wrecked infrastructure and disrupted channels of trade and communication. Progress slowed and was followed by retrogression. Arab elites, who in earlier times were known for their tolerance and love of learning, adopted a defensive, authoritarian conservatism; secular learning declined along with economic vitality. These tendencies were reinforced by centuries of Ottoman stagnation, and the fatalism and passivity associated with Islam in Western minds was the result.

In the present era, those regimes that have attempted to install command economies have done so in the name of justice and economic development. Among them, the results have been mixed; but with the rapid increase in oil wealth, the means are at hand whereby the region as a whole can progress through economic integration in a more liberal environment.

NOTES

1. H. A. R. Gibb, Mohammedanism, 2d ed. (New York: Oxford University Press, 1962), pp. 88-106.

2. Joseph Schacht, An Introduction to Islamic Law (London: Oxford University Press, 1964), pp. 76-78.

3. Koran, II, p. 275.

4. Phillip K. Hitti, History of the Arabs, 9th ed. (New York: St. Martin's Press, 1967), pp. 343-52.

5. Schacht, op. cit., pp. 78-79.

6. S. D. Goitein, A Mediterranean Society: Economic Foundations 1 (Berkeley: University of California Press, 1967).

7. Ibid., p. 170.

8. Ibid., pp. 245-47.

9. Ibid., pp. 230-40.

10. Ibid., pp. 241-43.

11. Ibid., pp. 247-48.

12. Schacht, op. cit., p. 39.

13. Goitein, op. cit., p. 203.

14. Ibid., p. 263.

15. Halil Inalcik, "Land Problems in Turkish History, "The Muslim World 45, no. 3 (July 1955): 221-24.

16. Stanford J. Shaw, The Financial and Administrative Organization and Development of Ottoman Egypt, 1517-1798 (Princeton, N.J.: Princeton University Press, 1962), p. 19.

17. Ibid., p. 68.

18. Halil Inalcik, "Bursa," The Encyclopaedia of Islam 1 (Leiden: E. J. Brill, 1960): 1333-36.

19. Bernard Lewis, The Emergence of Modern Turkey (London: Oxford University Press, 1965), p. 28.

20. Omer L. Barkan, "The Price Revolution of the Sixteenth Century: A Turning Point in the Economic History of the Near East," International Journal of Middle East Studies 6, no. 1 (January 1975): 8.

21. See, especially, Earl J. Hamilton, "American Treasure and the Rise of Capitalism (1500-1700)," Economica 2, no. 27 (November 1929): 338-57; and J. M. Keynes, A Treatise on Money (London: Macmillan, 1930): 2: 152-70.

22. Barkan, op. cit.

23. Barkan, op. cit., pp. 12-14.

24. Ibid., especially pp. 3, 4, and 28.

25. Omer C. Sarc, "Tanzimat ve Sanayimiz," in The Economic History of the Middle East, 1800-1914, ed. Charles Issawi (Chicago: University of Chicago Press, 1966), pp. 50-52.

26. W. S. Woytinsky and E. S. Woytinsky, World Commerce and Governments: Trends and Outlook (New York: Twentieth Century Fund, 1955), p. 439.

27. Ibid., p. 342.

28. Ibid., p. 195.

29. Peter Mansfield, Nasser's Egypt (Baltimore: Penguin Books, 1965), p. 54.

30. For the classic analysis of hydraulic totalitarianism, see Karl A. Wittfogel, Oriental Despotism: A Comparative Study of Total Power (New Haven, Conn.: Yale University Press, 1957).

31. Patrick O'Brien, The Revolution in Egypt's Economic System (London: Oxford University Press, 1966), pp. 85-103.

32. Ibid., p. 126.

33. Harvey H. Smith, et al., Area Handbook for the United Arab Republic, Prepared for Department of the Army by the American University, DA Pam 550-43 (Washington, D.C.: Government Printing Office, 1970), p. 228.

3

DESIGNS FOR PROGRESS

At the present time, all of the governments of the Middle East are engaged in strenuous efforts to accelerate the pace of economic development. In most cases, this endeavor involves the use of economic plans and institutional reforms designed to increase the availability of economic resources and to improve the proportions in which they are combined in production. Well-conceived and -executed plans and institutional reforms can increase the rate of growth and lead to general betterment. Obversely, poorly conceived and badly executed designs can waste resources and create general discontent.

LAND REFORM

Among the institutional changes undertaken, land reform is certainly among the more pervasive and important. Land reform has been undertaken by such politically divergent states as socialist Syria and Iraq and conservative Iran. Since changes in the distribution of property rights influence worker productivity, income distribution, and the savings rate, land reform can have profound economic consequences regardless of the political system involved. The basic importance of agricultural conditions in the Middle East is made clear when one considers labor's heavy reliance upon agriculture as a source of employment. (See Table 7.3.)

A prosperous and expanding agricultural sector can play an important role in a country's development. As the Ottoman authorities recognized so well, agriculture is a basic source of tax revenue. In the era of Western penetration, Middle Eastern agriculture became the major source of foreign exchange. Modern governments recognize that the role of agriculture extends beyond government revenue and exchange generation. Agriculture can provide a mass market for industrial products and contribute to the savings necessary for capital formation. It is the obvious source of food for the industrial labor force and urban population. Finally, agricultural labor is the pool from which industrial workers are drawn. The potential for balanced economic development is enhanced, therefore, by agricultural development.

As the disintegration of the Ottoman Empire accelerated in the late nineteenth century, local property laws evolved in different ways; and this produced diversity in patterns of land tenure arrangements among countries. In Egypt, private ownership of land developed, so that, by the twentieth century, virtually all agricultural land was in private hands. The combination of private property and the Muslim inheritance law, however, tended to produce a fragmentation of holdings into small plots, but the owners of large estates were able to maintain their holdings intact by the use of private foundations. The result was a highly unequal distribution of property rights. Before the beginning of land reform in 1952, 94 percent of Egyptian agricultural holdings were of five acres or less, and these accounted for only 35 percent of the total agricultural land area. At the same time, the 12 largest holdings, or 0.004 percent of all holdings, represented 36 percent of the total agricultural area. [1]

In Iraq and Syria, most of the agricultural land remained technically state land. In practice, land came increasingly under the control of tribal sheikhs and absentee landlords, who paid rent to the state but operated large holdings as private estates. Land was rented by the de facto proprietors to peasants or exploited by sharecropping arrangements. In Iraq, these developments also produced a highly lopsided distribution of effective property rights. Before the reform process began in 1958, 68 percent of the land in private hands was in holdings of more than 600 acres and owned by only 2 percent of the proprietors. At the other extreme, 68 percent of the proprietors owned 3.3 percent of the land in holdings of 18 acres or less. [2] The state owned 23 percent of cultivable land in 1958.

European colonization produced similar effects in the Maghreb states, especially in Algeria, where French settlers acquired the best agricultural land. Before the withdrawal of the French, 2.3 percent of the proprietors owned 40 percent of the aggregate agricultural area, while 69 percent owned 15 percent. There is evidence of a similar skewness in the distributions of property rights in the agricultural sections of Morocco and Tunisia. [3]

When the distribution of property rights is highly unequal, land reform usually involves the dividing of large estates among peasant cultivators. By combining ownership and use, cultivators are given a proprietary incentive to use resources efficiently to save and invest

in order to increase their own productivity. When reform is combined
with programs designed to provide agricultural processing, storage,
marketing, and credit facilities, the goal of increased agricultural
output can be realized.

Assuming that large estates utilize more capital-intensive techniques of production than do smaller ones, the redistribution of large
estates among formerly landless farmers will tend to increase the
employment of labor. Furthermore, as long as the level of real output is maintained, the elimination or reduction of land rents paid by
tenant farmers will reduce real income inequality. This, in turn,
should increase the effective demand for domestically produced subsistence goods and reduce the demand for any luxury goods imported
by the landlord class. Conceptually, at least, reform can contribute
to greater social justice, increased employment, and domestic economic development.

Land reform is sometimes pursued primarily for political reasons. In preindustrial economies, land is closely associated with
political power. In some cases, land reform has been used to reduce
the power of conservative political groups, although a regime's political gain may come at the expense of agricultural productivity.

It is important to recognize that the economic goals—higher productivity, increased employment, and greater income equality—are
not automatically achieved by land reform legislation. Much depends
on the smoothness and timing of the property transfer process and on
the adequacy of modern capital resources available to the cultivators
after reform. The contrasting outcomes of the major reform experi-
ments make this clear.

Of the major land reform programs in the Middle East, Egypt's
provides the most evidence of unambiguous success. The objectives
of the Egyptian reform were to break the political power of the established landlord class, to consolidate fragmented holdings, to increase
the productivity of land, and to increase peasant incomes, as well as
to encourage cooperatives and to upgrade other cooperant factors of
production. In most of these respects, there are clear indications of
success.

The Agrarian Reform Law of 1952 established a limit of 200 feddan (208 acres) an individual might own; in 1969, this was reduced to
50 feddan. Despite the fact that only about one-sixth of the land was
affected, the reform succeeded in a significant redistribution of property rights. By 1965, 94 percent of the landowners held 57 percent
of the cultivated area, while the relevant share in 1952 had been 35
percent.[4] Although the damaged landlords were compensated with
nonnegotiable government bonds, the state ultimately reneged on these
obligations, and the bonds became worthless. In addition to politically
disarming the once powerful landlords, the government's program for

cooperatives was quantitatively achieved. From a base of 1,700 in 1952, the number of farmers' organizations had increased threefold by the mid-1960s.

It is impossible to measure the net welfare effects of these changes by weighing the utility gains of those helped against the losses of those hurt. It is nevertheless important to note that the reform was accompanied by steady gains in the productivity of land used for major crops. During the two decades between 1950 and 1970, maize yields increased by 80 percent and wheat yields by 50 percent, while cotton and barley yields increased by 44 and 23 percent, respectively. [5] Given these productivity gains and the reduction in cash rents produced by the reform program, real farm income must have risen.

Although modest in its scope, Egypt's agrarian reform program was relatively successful because its objectives were within the country's administrative and technical capabilities. The extensive structure of farmers' cooperatives provided a mechanism for allocating credit, seeds, fertilizers, and insecticides according to the government's overall agricultural production program. The cooperatives also provided the institutional arrangements for marketing the major commercial crops. Egypt's long experience in water resource management and its relatively large supply of modern agronomists contributed to the implementation of the land reform program. However, these ingredients of success were not equally available elsewhere in the Middle East.

The union of Syria and Egypt in the United Arab Republic in 1958 brought Egyptian-style land reform to Syria, a country where agricultural conditions are quite different. Rather than having to deal with relentless population pressure on relatively fixed land, Syria's essential problem is the failure to utilize its agricultural potential. Typically, one-quarter to one-third of the cultivable area is left fallow. Furthermore, the total area of cultivation can be expanded. Although Egyptian agriculture depends entirely on irrigation, no more than 10 percent of the cultivated area in Syria was irrigated in the 1960s. This reliance on dry farming and the variability of rainfall contribute to wide variations in crop yields and uncertainty in agricultural planning. Egypt's strength lies in its long tradition of cooperative agricultural endeavor built around control of the Nile, while Syria's best hope for development lies in a social policy designed to harness the energies of its entrepreneurs without debilitating or destroying them.

Syria has a long tradition of commercial astuteness, and, in the postwar era, the energies of its merchant-capitalists turned to agriculture. In response to world price incentives, cotton output increased nearly 11-fold between 1945 and 1953, as the area devoted to cotton expanded from 43,000 to 116,000 acres. In this eight-year period, the total cultivated area increased from 5.66 million to 9.07 million acres, an annual compound rate of increase of 6 percent. In that period, wheat and barley output just about doubled. [6] These remarkable gains were produced largely by the exploitation of hitherto uncropped land, mostly in the Jezira region, from Aleppo to the Iraqi border. Utilizing tractors, pumps, and extensive farming techniques, the entrepreneurs of Aleppo extended cultivation to these new lands leased from tribal sheikhs. This postwar agricultural development created a division in agricultural conditions in Syria. Capital-intensive techniques employed in the newly developed areas resulted in relatively low man/land ratios; population densities were higher relative to land in the old agricultural areas around Homs and Hama, where traditional techniques and sharecropping arrangements were typical.

Although population pressure on the land was less in Syria than in Egypt and disparity in the size distribution of agricultural holdings was less, perhaps half of the agricultural households in the old settled areas owned no land at all. [7] Given the high rents charged tenants, as much as 75 percent of the crop, there was an equity case to be made for some resettlement of population as owner-operators on the new lands of the Jezira and on state land.

Syria's reform law of 1958 provided for the expropriation of private land and the redistribution of this and state land to landless peasants. Variations in the maximum size of holdings permitted were tailored to water supply and the pattern of crop production. Broadly speaking, the law limited individual holdings to a range of 80 to 300 hectares. In addition, the law and subsequent amendments provided for the redistribution of land in plots of 8 to 30 hectares and for the establishment of agricultural cooperatives. As in the Egyptian case, credit and other necessary services would be provided through the cooperatives. Unlike Egypt, where plots were combined and managed in large units, under the Syrian reform program, holdings were to be managed individually.

In application, Syria's land reform program suffered from political instability, the failure of the cooperative movement to develop, producer disincentives, and other technical and administrative deficiencies. After initial moves began in 1958, reform was suspended in 1961 with the breaking of the union with Egypt, reintroduced in 1962, and given new emphasis by the resurgent Ba'thists after 1963. As late as 1967, only 30 percent of the land subject to the reform program had been redistributed. [8]

The delays in implementation created suspicion of the government's intentions and uncertainty as to the ultimate distribution of land. This uncertainty is reflected in a steady decline in real net fixed capital formation in agriculture after 1963. Agricultural real investment declined from £S 100 million in 1963 to £S 15 million in 1968 (at

1963 prices).[9] Uncertainty, the slow development of the cooperative movement, and controlled grain prices set too low in relation to costs served to discourage production at the margin, so that the cultivated area also declined from 1963 to the end of the decade.[10] On the other hand, the yields of major crops in years of adequate rainfall were maintained. Wheat yields were as good in the 1960s as they were in the years of 1948-52. Average barley yields were slightly higher, and cotton yields on irrigated land rose significantly. Evidently, these gains were offset by the decline in the area of cultivation; the Food and Agricultural Organization of the United Nations (FAO) agricultural production indexes show a declining trend from 1964 through 1970.

In view of these difficulties, the government pushed to complete the redistribution process in the late 1960s. According to Table 3.1, in the period 1958-69, 3.7 million acres were expropriated and 3.1 million were allocated to farmers. Thus, the process was over 80 percent complete by 1970, in the sense that nearly as much land had been returned to the private sector as had been absorbed by the public sector. Most of the land distributed, however, was state land. It appears, therefore, that a considerable potential for distributing property to landless peasants remained at that time, since only 29 percent

TABLE 3.1

Land Distribution, Egypt, Syria, and Iraq

			Land Distribution		
		Expropri-	Expropri-	State	Number of
		ated Land	ated Land	Land	Families
Country	Period	(acres)	(acres)	(acres)	Affected
Egypt	1952-66	980,346	763,249	—	303,624
Syria	1958-69	3,738,623	1,069,118	2,023,349	102,238
Iraq	1958-72	5,656,735	1,530,010	1,165,498	104,739

Sources: M. R. El Ghonemy, "Economic and Institutional Organization of Egyptian Agriculture since 1952," in Egypt Since the Revolution, ed. P. J. Vatikiotis (New York: Praeger, 1968), pp. 71-72; United Nations, Economic and Social Office in Beirut, Studies on Selected Development Problems in Various Countries in the Middle East, 1971 (New York: United Nations, 1971), p. 37; and Iraq, Central Statistical Organization, Annual Abstract of Statistics, 1972 (Baghdad: Ministry of Planning, 1972), pp. 85-88.

of the land expropriated had actually been distributed. All property taken, of course, should not necessarily be returned to use—for example, marginal land that is vulnerable to erosion when plowed should be reserved for pasture or left idle.

The contrast between the Egyptian and Syrian experiences demonstrates the importance of keeping goals within the capabilities of the bureaucracy. In spite of its lower level of capability, the Syrian government undertook the reallocation of nearly four times as much land as had the Egyptians. Consequently, the quantity of arable and permanently cropped land in Syria declined by 12 percent between 1964 and 1973, so that the net result seems to have been a loss of potential output.

The Iraqi experience was somewhat different. Iraq's reform law of 1958 set an upper limit on the ownership of irrigated land of 1,000 donums (618 acres) and a limit of 2,000 on rain-watered land. Land over these limits was to be expropriated and distributed with state land to cultivators in plots of 30 to 120 donums. As in Egypt and Syria, cooperatives were to provide the factors of production formerly supplied by the landlords.

The government's task was enormous. In the period 1958-72, it acquired 5.7 million acres, half again as much as the government expropriated in Syria and nearly six times as much as in Egypt. In practice, the government's ability to expropriate far exceeded its capacity to redistribute. Expropriation ran so far ahead of distribution that, by the mid-1960s, the state had become a superlandlord, with nearly 200,000 tenants under its supervision. By 1972, after 14 years of reform, only 48 percent of the quantity taken had been returned to owner-operators.

As one might expect, productivity declined just after the initiation of the reform process. Per hectare yields of wheat, barley, rice, and cotton were lower in 1959-63 than they were in 1954-58. Similarly, the area of cultivation of all crops except wheat declined, as did the production of each of these main crops. But the period of 1959-63 was one of drought in the area, so that the productivity of rain-watered land would have suffered in any event. FAO figures support the impression of agricultural improvement in the later 1960s. The average yields of wheat, rice, and cotton were higher in 1967-71 than in the earlier reform years. Production and cultivation were also higher for wheat, rice, and cotton. Per capita food and agricultural production indexes also suggest improving general conditions in the period 1966-69.

The reason for the apparent recovery of Iraqi agriculture in the 1960s appears to lie in the improvement of the government's performance in several aspects of the reform program after 1965. In that year, the program was incorporated into the country's five-year plan, which would tend to provide for better coordination of policies. In the later 1960s, the cooperative movement was greatly strengthened. The number of registered cooperatives rose from under 100 in 1965 to over 800 by the early 1970s. At the same time, the supply of cooperant factors, especially fertilizers and tractors, was increased. The use of commercial fertilizers had been negligible or nonexistent prior to this time. Thus, the Iraqi government's record in agriculture is mixed. It appears that its positive contribution is offsetting the negative aspects of the reform program. In the end, it seems likely that collective farming on de facto public estates may become the norm in Iraq. The ideological basis of policy points in this direction. In the long run, sustained improvement in agriculture in Iraq depends on dealing successfully with the land salinity problem through the development of a better drainage system in the irrigated areas.

In the three reforms considered thus far, Egypt's was in response to the most pressing need, as the burden of population on the land was far greater there. With relatively fixed supplies of land and little or no unutilized potential, the need to maintain agricultural employment and to provide production and investment incentives in agriculture was more critical. The factor-proportions problem of Egypt can be seen in the relation between families benefited and land distributed. Given the data presented in Table 3.1, the average number of acres distributed per family in Egypt was 2.5, whereas in Syria and Iraq, 30 and 26 acres, respectively, were distributed per family. In Egypt, a larger number received a smaller amount of land, reflecting the higher man/land ratio there.

Although the reform programs of Syria and Iraq were applications of the Egyptian model, Iran's agrarian reform was a pragmatic Iranian formula. Population settlement in Iran, as elsewhere in the Middle East, depends on the availability of relatively scarce water resources. Consequently, rural settlement tends to be in villages rather than on isolated or scattered farms, and village land is divided among farmers in terms of plowlands—that is, amounts of land that a yoke of oxen can cultivate.

Prior to the recent reform, the distribution of landed property reflected a medieval rewards system. In Persia, as in Ottoman lands, military officers and others were awarded rights in land or its revenue stream in recognition of services rendered the government. Although peasants might own their own houses, control over land gave the holders of large estates authority over the peasants and their villages. As a result, local power tended to accrue to the owners of large estates. These large landowners formed the ruling class, made up of members of the royal family, government officials, tribal chiefs, religious leaders, and wealthy merchants, who were able to buy property. When property rights were traded, villages and peasants were

effectively included in the transaction. Sharecropping was the typical
connection between the landlord and the peasant, with relative shares
in revenue reflecting the shares of each in the supply of the necessary
factors of production: land, water, seeds, oxen, and labor. In addition to private landownership, the state and the religious foundations
also controlled landed property. The distribution of property was un-
known to reform, as no cadastral survey had been made.[11]

On the eve of land reform, Iran was saddled with a social structure inappropriate for modern economic development, that is, a ruling
class opposed to social reform, a disgruntled peasantry, and dissatisfied modernizers unable to effectuate change. Agricultural development, the key to improved rural welfare, was impeded by a lack of
water, poor seeds, antiquated implements, and traditional technology.
Also contributing to static agriculture was the inadequacy of rural
transportation and communications systems. Furthermore, the pattern of ownership provided little or no incentive for the cultivators to
improve their own productivity.

In 1962, a land reform law was passed that limited ownership
to one village, compensated landlords on the basis of the property
taxes they paid, and made membership in a cooperative obligatory
for those peasants receiving land. Most of those who voted for the
land reform bill failed to realize its implications and voted for it under the assumption that it would not be enforced.[12] This first phase
of land reform was implemented to the benefit of some 787,000 families. (See Table 3.2.) A relatively small fraction of the total number

TABLE 3.2

Property Redistribution, Iran, 1962–71

| Period | Property Redistributed | | Number of Families Affected |
	Villages (acres)	Farms (acres)	
1962–64, Phase 1	16,593	—	787,000
1965–71 Phases 2 and 3	54,849	21,838	2,518,000

Source: Bank Markazi Iran, Annual Report and Balance Sheet,
1973 (Tehran: BMI, 1973), p. 192.

of villages was affected, so that, once started, the process of reform had to be continued lest unrest spread among the majority of the peasants who had not benefited. In order to reach the peasants attached to the property of small landlords owning one village or less, a second phase of reform was instituted three years later.

Under Phase 2, landlords who were not affected by Phase 1 were required either to lease their land to the occupying peasants or to divide land between themselves and the peasants in proportion to the income shares provided for under existing sharecropping arrangements. It was found that, even after these requirements had been enforced, well over 1 million farmers still lacked legal title to their land, as landlords evidently preferred to lease property rather than to sell. A new law, therefore, was passed in 1968, which required that property being leased on a long-term basis be offered for sale to the lessees. The implementation of this law led to the announcement in September 1971 that the reform program had been completed and that there was no farmer who did not own the land he worked.

In the process of reform, the cooperative movement had been greatly increased, and by 1975 nearly 3,000 cooperative societies had been established, with a membership of 2.6 million farmers. In an effort to increase mechanization, 65 joint stock companies were in operation, with over 20,000 shareholders at that time.

The distinctive feature of the Iranian reform is its pragmatic, undoctrinaire approach to solving an extremely important but politically sensitive social problem. As Table 3.2 suggests, well over 3 million farmers have benefited from the phased reform program; and apparently no village has gone unaffected. Although the role of the landlord class has been eroded, the development of the cooperative network is providing a mechanism by which the cooperant factors of production can be supplied and improved.

The long-term effects of land reform in Iran are as yet unclear. Although modest growth in the production of the main crops continues, there is little evidence of substantial improvement in agriculture's ability to meet the needs of the population.

In the final analysis, the results of land reform in the Middle East are mixed. In all of the cases considered here, the power of landlords was reduced, and the resulting reductions in land rents must have contributed to higher real incomes for farming families. But none of these solutions represents a durable answer to the problem of rapid population growth; as in most cases, population growth is nullifying output increases. From 1969 to 1975, secular trends in per capita agricultural output were negative in Egypt and Iraq, unchanged in Iran, and slightly positive in Syria, where greater pragmatism in agricultural policy served to reduce the earlier confusion surrounding its land reform program.

Of the major cases of land reform, Egypt's was the most capably conducted, utilizing as it did the government's experience in water resource management, its developed market structure, its agricultural technicians, and its long tradition of public-private cooperation in agriculture. The problems of Iraq and Syria arose from a lack of the necessary administrative assets to attain the goals set. Iran's reform process was smoother because it limited its objectives in proportion to its capabilities in a step-by-step approach.

After reform, all of the countries still face their perennial problems, as well as certain new ones. Egypt must continue to cope with shortages of agricultural resources in relation to labor, as well as the accelerated waterlogging of the land. Iraq has yet to deal adequately with its salinity problem, and it has thus far failed to find a system of management as effective as that formerly provided by the tribal sheikhs. Syria's need to make more efficient use of its agricultural resources continues. Iran still faces the problem of inadequate marketing facilities, shortages of water, and the need to improve agricultural technology. In addition, land reform itself has served to make 80 percent of its farms inefficiently small. Thus, land reform is no panacea, but it may be a necessary condition in the long run for agricultural development. In the end, there is an obvious need for a sustained agricultural policy that is both consistent with a nation's long-term economic goals and within the limits of its resource endowment.

ECONOMIC PLANNING

To the majority of its proponents, national economic planning essentially means rational decision making by government—that is, the selection of specific goals and the design of a program or strategy for achieving them. By this broad definition, virtually all governments plan. It is difficult to find a state that is not pursuing a particular mix of monetary, fiscal, and commercial policies designed to attain certain specified objectives. This definition is too broad to be useful. It is more worthwhile to draw a distinction between those governments that are officially committed to detailed national plans and those that are not. Governments may be said to be engaged in planning if they are committed to attempting to shape the broad pattern of future economic development along lines announced in advance.

National plans usually aim to accelerate the rate of economic growth beyond that which otherwise would occur. From this goal follows an implied commitment to structural change and institutional reform. The conditions of economic backwardness usually make reform an essential concomitant to internally generated economic growth.

Feudalistic land tenure systems, illiteracy, tax inequities, market imperfection, inadequate administrative systems, and excessive social stratification provide disincentives that must be offset if faster growth is to occur. The resulting broad process of change is implied by the term <u>modernization</u>.[13] A national planning document represents a collection of ends, means, and strategies, often presented on the basis of sectoral programs, which are intended to facilitate growth and modernization. Plans often include specification of growth targets and other objectives to be achieved during the planning period, as well as the individual projects prepared for implementation in the pursuit of the sectoral targets. Internally consistent plans balance resources that are available against resource requirements.

In mixed economies, private economic decision making continues alongside public decision making. The authorities forecast private savings and investment decisions and take them into account when specifying targets and goals. Private decisions may be influenced indirectly through monetary and fiscal policies or directly through exchange controls, licensing, quotas, and rationing.

Planning documents reflect a wide range of comprehensiveness and sophistication. In general, planning tends to become more quantitative in method with the passage of time. First plans may be largely qualitative outlines of a government's objectives and priorities, with available resources only loosely related to their uses. Subsequent plans may be substantially quantitative, with input-output tables to assure resource balance and econometric optimization models for maximizing returns to resources.

Theorists and practitioners of planning have evolved three basic criteria that may be used in appraising the quality of a plan: comprehensiveness, consistency, and optimality.[14]

To satisfy the comprehensiveness requirement, a plan should include a set of output and income targets to be attained during the plan period. Further, it should quantitatively trace the growth in the inputs needed for the attainment of the growth targets. Consistency requires the demonstration of balance between the anticipated demands and supplies of labor and capital and other resources, both in the aggregate and on a sectoral basis. Beyond the comprehensiveness and consistency requirements, a plan should attempt to demonstrate that, in fulfillment, it would make the best possible use of society's resources.

These theoretical criteria are extremely rigorous and are not likely to be completely satisfied in any real planning situation. It is safe to say that the optimality criterion is never satisfied in practice. In the Middle East, plans appear to meet the comprehensiveness requirement more closely than they do the other criteria.

Economic planning in the Middle East rests, in most cases, on Harrod-Domar foundations. Sectoral incremental capital/output ratios

(ICORs) are estimated from past experience, and the volume of investment required to produce a target rate of growth is thereby ascertained. Input-output tables are frequently used to check the consistency of plans, by projecting resources and their uses to the end of the planning periods. Although the private sector is subject to manipulation through systems of rewards and penalties, planning targets for this sector are usually indicative—that is, measures of how the economy is expected to behave, given the conditions assumed during the planning period. In all of the countries of the area, the magnitude and variety of economic statistics increased during the 1960s. Virtually all governments are now supplied with national accounts, survey data, and sectoral studies.

Tables 3.3 and 3.4 provide comparisons of target rates of growth in real product with estimates of actual growth rates, but such comparisons do not constitute a meaningful test of planning effectiveness. Comparisons based on the tables serve only as measures of the extent to which the declared aspirations of the planners were fulfilled in reality. The best test of the efficacy of planning is a comparison of the results under planning with what would have occurred without it, but such comparisons are obviously conjectural.

Recent growth performances in the Middle East reflect the prevailing pattern of resource distribution. Achieved rates of growth are generally faster among the oil states, and their performances tend more nearly to equal or exceed expectations. During the time period covered, achieved rates of growth of less than 5 percent per annum occurred only among the nonoil states. Other important differences are apparent as well. Nonoil states are hampered in their development by relatively low savings propensities, while high savings ratios occur among the oil states. Investment usually exceeds national savings among the nonoil states, but several of the oil states are capital exporters. Although particular nonoil states, such as Syria and Turkey, have sustained good growth performances over long periods of time, the greater potential for rapid income growth lies with the oil states. Rising petroleum output and/or unit prices mean increasing government revenue. Increased government spending can lead to faster real growth in nonoil sectors, either directly through government investment or indirectly through expenditures that raise disposable personal incomes, savings, and private capital formation.

This process, however, has definite limits. Because development is such a recent phenomenon, the major oil states have severely circumscribed capacities to absorb additional capital. Road transport systems, communications networks, and other forms of infrastructure are typically rudimentary. Technical expertise and managerial skills are in short supply. Under these circumstances, massive spending by the government can quickly lead to runaway inflation and economic

TABLE 3.3

Plans and Performance: Major Middle Eastern Oil States

Country	Period	Compound Annual Rate of Real Output Growth	Savings Ratio[a]	Gross Investment Ratio[b]
Algeria				
Target (GDP)	1970–73	9.0	—	—
Actual (GDP)	1970–73	5.7	.32	.40
Target (GDP)	1974–77	10.0	—	—
Actual (GDP)	1974–76	6.0	.45	.51
Iran				
Target (GNP)	1963–67	6.0	—	—
Actual (GNP)	1963–67	9.7	.16	.18
Target (GNP)	1968–72	9.3	—	—
Actual (GNP)	1968–72	10.8	.20	.22
Target (GNP)	1973	11.4	—	—
Target (GNP)	1974–77	25.9	—	—
Actual (GNP)	1974–76	9.3	.41	.26
Iraq				
Target (GNP)	1965–69	8.0	—	—
Actual (GNP)	1965–69	6.2	.20	.17
Target (GNP)	1970–74	7.1	—	—
Actual (GNP)	1970–74	6.3	.32	.21
Kuwait				
Target (GDP)	1968–72	6.5	—	—
Actual (GDP)	1968–72	5.5	.48	.18
Actual (GDP)	1973–76	5.8	.69	.07
Libya				
Target (GDP)	1973–75	10.7	—	—
Actual (GDP)	1973–75	17.0	.37	.32
Saudi Arabia				
Target (GDP)	1971–75	9.8	—	—
Actual (GDP)	1971–75	13.5	.58	.15
Target (GDP)	1975–80	10.2	—	—

[a]Refers to the mean of annual ratios of gross national savings to GNP.
[b]Refers to the mean of annual ratios of gross domestic investment to GNP.

Sources: Algeria—Le Conseil des Ministres, Plan Quadriennal, 1970–1973: Rapport General (Alger: Republique Algerienne Democratique et Populaire, 1970); Le Conseil des Ministres, II Plan Quadriennal, 1974-1977: Rapport General (Alger: Republique Algerienne Democratique et Populaire, 1974). Iran—Plan Organization, Third Plan, 1341–1346 (Tehran: Division of Economic Affairs, Government of Iran, 1961); Plan Organization, Fourth Plan, 1968–1972 (Tehran: Imperial Government of Iran, 1968); Plan Organization, The Fifth Plan, Echo-Iran Trade and Industry Publication, Supplement no. 200 (Tehran, March 1973). Iraq—Council of Ministers, The Five Years Economic Plan, 1965–1969, Law no. 87 of 1965 (Baghdad: Government of Iraq, 1965); Iraq Planning Board, The General Outline of the Five Year Economic and Social Development Plan of Iraq, 1970–1974 (Baghdad: Government of Iraq, 1970). Kuwait—Planning Board, The First Five Year Development Plan, 1967/68-1971/72 (Kuwait: PB, 1967). Libya—Planning Council, Three Year Economic and Social Development Plan: 1973–1975 (Tripoli: PC, 1972). Saudi Arabia—Central Planning Organization, Development Plan 1390 A.H. (Riyadh: Government of Saudi Arabia, 1970); United States—Saudi Arabian Joint Commission on Economic Cooperation, Summary of Saudi Arabian Five Year Development Plan, 1975–1980 (Washington, D.C.: Department of the Treasury, 1975).

Actual ratios and growth rates were calculated on the basis of data found in International Bank for Reconstruction and Development, World Tables, 1975 (Washington, D.C.: IBRD, 1976); International Monetary Fund, International Financial Statistics (Washington, D.C.: IMF), various issues; and International Bank for Reconstruction and Development, "Economic Data Sheet I—National Accounts and Prices," mimeographed (Washington, D.C.: IBRD, 1978).

TABLE 3.4

Plans and Performance: Middle Eastern States without Major Oil Resources

Country	Period	Compound Annual Rate of Real Output Growth	Savings Ratio[a]	Gross Investment Ratio[b]
Egypt				
Target (GDP)	1960–64	7.2	—	—
Actual (GDP)	1960–64	6.6	.12	.16
Actual (GDP)	1965–71	3.6	.10	.15
Actual (GDP)	1972–76	6.2	.06	.19
Israel				
Target (GNP)	1971–75	7.5	—	—
Actual (GNP)	1971–73	10.0	.11	.31
Actual (GNP)	1974–76	2.9	.03	.30
Jordan				
Target (GNP)	1964–70	7.3	—	—
Actual (GNP)	1964–70	4.8	−.04	.18
Target (GDP)	1973–75	8.0	—	—
Actual (GDP)	1973–75	4.3	.00	.23
Lebanon				
Target (GDP)	1972–77	7.0	—	—
Actual (GDP)	1972–73	8.3	.19	.24
Morocco				
Target (GNP)	1960–64	6.2	—	—
Actual (GNP)	1960–64	3.2	.10	.11
Target (GNP)	1965–67	3.5	—	—
Actual (GNP)	1965–67	2.4	.09	.12
Target (GNP)	1968–72	4.3	—	—
Actual (GNP)	1968–72	6.2	.12	.15
Target (GNP)	1973–77	7.5	—	—
Actual (GNP)	1973–76	5.8	.15	.19
Sudan				
Target (GDP)	1961–70	5.2	—	—
Actual (GDP)	1961–70	1.3	.12	.15
Target (GDP)	1971–75	7.6	—	—
Actual (GDP)	1971–75	5.7	.09	.12
Syria				
Target (NDP)	1961–65	7.2	—	—
Actual (GDP)	1961–65	8.5	.12	.14
Target (NDP)	1966–70	7.2	—	—
Actual (GDP)	1966–70	4.8	.11	.14
Target (NDP)	1971–75	8.2	—	—
Actual (GDP)	1971–75	6.2	.17	.23
Tunisia				
Target (GDP)	1965–68	6.5	—	—
Actual (GDP)	1965–68	4.3	.14	.26
Target (GDP)	1969–72	6.5	—	—
Actual (GDP)	1969–72	10.6	.17	.22
Target (GDP)	1973–76	6.6	—	—
Actual (GDP)	1973–76	7.6	.23	.27

Country	Period	Compound Annual Rate of Real Output Growth	Savings Ratio[a]	Gross Investment Ratio[b]
Turkey				
Target (GNP)	1963-67	7.0	—	—
Actual (GNP)	1963-67	6.7	.16	.18
Target (GNP)	1968-72	7.0	—	—
Actual (GNP)	1968-72	7.0	.19	.21
Target (GNP)	1973-77	7.9	—	—
Actual (GNP)	1973-76	7.2	.18	.21

[a]Refers to the mean of annual ratios of gross national savings to GNP.
[b]Refers to the mean of annual ratios of gross domestic investment to GNP.

Sources: Egypt—National Planning Committee, General Frame of the 5-Year Plan for Economic and Social Development, 1960-1965 (Cairo: NPC, 1960). Israel—Economic Planning Authority, Development Plan for the National Economy, 1971-1975 (Jerusalem: EPA, 1969). Jordan—Jordan Development Board, The Seven Year Plan for Economic Development of Jordan, 1964-70 (Amman: JDB, 1965); National Planning Council, Three Year Development Plan, 1973-75 (Amman: NPC, 1972). Lebanon—Ministere du Plan, Plan Sexennal de Developpement, 1972-1977 (Beirut: Republique Libanaise). Morocco—Division de la Coordination Economique et du Plan, Plan Quinquennal, 1960-64 (Rabat, 1960); Economic Coordination and Planning Division, Three Year Plan, 1965-1967 (Rabat: Royal Cabinet, 1965); Division de la Coordination Economique et du Plan, Plan Quinquennal, 1968-1972 (Rabat: Ministere des Affaires Economiques du Plan et de la Formation des Cadres, 1968); Direction du Plan et du Developpement Regional, Plan de Developpement Economique et Social, 1973-1977 (Rabat: Secretariat D'Etat au Plan au Developpement Regional et a la Formation des Cadres, 1973). Sudan—Economic Planning Secretariat, The Ten Year Plan of Economic and Social Development, 1961/62-1970/71 (Khartoum: EPS, 1962); Ministry of Planning, The Five Year Plan for Economic and Social Development, 1970/71-1974/75 (Khartoum: Government of the Democratic Republic of the Sudan, 1970). Syria—Ministry of Planning, The Syrian Five-Year Plan for Economic and Social Development, 1960/61-1964/65 (Damascus: Government of the Syrian Arab Republic, 1961); Ministere du Plan, Le Second Plan Quinquennal de la Republique Arabe Syrienne, 1966-1970 (Damas: Centre D'Etudes et Documentations, 1966); Ministry of Planning, Third Five-Year Plan for Economic and Social Development, 1971-1975 (Damascus: Arab Office for Press and Documentation, 1971). Tunisia—Secretariat D'Etat au Plan et a L'Economie Nationale, Plan Quadriennal, 1965-1968 (Tunis: Government de la Republique Tunisienne, 1965); Secretariat D'Etat au Plan et a L'Economie Nationale, Plan de Developpement Economique et Social, 1969-1972 (Tunis: Government de la Republique Tunisienne, 1969); IV Plan de Developpement et Social, 1973-1976 (Tunis: Government de la Republique Tunisienne, 1973). Turkey—State Planning Organization, First Five Year Development Plan, 1963-1967 (Ankara: Prime Ministry of the Turkish Republic, 1963); State Planning Organization, Second Five Year Development Plan, 1968-1972 (Ankara: Central Bank of the Republic of Turkey, 1969); State Planning Organization, A Summary of the Third Five Year Development Plan, 1973-1977 (Ankara: Prime Ministry of the Republic of Turkey, 1973).

Actual growth rates were calculated on the basis of data found in International Bank for Reconstruction and Development, World Tables, 1975 (Washington, D.C.: IBRD, 1976); International Monetary Fund, International Financial Statistics (Washington, D.C.: IMF), various issues; and International Bank for Reconstruction and Development, "Economic Data Sheet I—National Accounts and Prices," mimeographed (Washington, D.C.: IBRD, 1978).

chaos. Inadequate port facilities have been a particularly troublesome bottleneck. The Middle Eastern oil states are heavily dependent on imports for both consumption and capital formation, so that increased government spending is immediately reflected in increased demand for imports. With inadequate port facilities, the stream of real imports may not keep abreast of spending for imports. Mounting congestion costs are reflected in domestic prices.* Delays lengthen the gestation periods of projects, upsetting time-frame planning and contributing to cost overruns. Relative prices are altered, and differential burdens are inequitably imposed on different classes of consumers. Although Middle Eastern governments have adopted elaborate import subsidy schemes to protect the living standards of the poorer classes,

---

*The inflationary potential of inadequate port facilities can be appreciated by considering the number of days spent queuing by ships in the Middle Eastern ports as of September 1976.

Location	Days
Gulf and elsewhere	
Abu Dhabi (United Arab Emirates)	22–24
Bahrain	50–55
Basrah (Iraq)	60–90
Bandar Shapur (Iran)	40–160
Bushir (Iran)	40–145
Damman (Saudi Arabia)	80–120
Dubai (United Arab Emirates)	30–40
Khorramshahr (Iran)	60–200
Kuwait	15–50
Elsewhere	
Algiers	2
Alexandria	2
Casablanca	0
Jiddah (Saudi Arabia)	25–30

Assuming that the opportunity cost of keeping a general cargo vessel waiting to unload was $4,000 a day in 1976, and that the average vessel had to wait 60 days in Gulf ports to discharge 2,000 tons of cargo, port congestion would have added $120 to the cost of each ton handled. Such extra congestion costs are ultimately passed on to domestic producers and consumers, either directly through demurrage or congestion surcharges or indirectly through higher freight rates.

the pace of inflation since 1973 has eroded the efficacy of these subsidies. (See Table 4.10.)

With the sharp increase in oil prices in 1973, the major exporters revised their development expectations accordingly. Iran, for instance, raised the overall growth target of its fifth plan (1973-77) from
11.4 to 25.9 percent a year, while doubling its cumulative investment
target. While programs do address themselves to the problem of inadequate infrastructure, they simultaneously seek rapid industrialization and a general increase in capital intensity. The second Saudi
Arabian plan seems to represent the ambitions, problems, and possibilities of the oil states on a grand scale. Although conditions vary
among these states, an appreciation of the Saudi situation provides
insight into planning problems in other petroleum-exporting countries.

The broad economic goals of the Saudi Arabian Second Five-
Year Development Plan (1975-80) include the generation of a high annual rate of growth (10.2 percent), the diversification of the economy
to reduce dependence on oil, the development of human resources and
individual welfare, and the development of the infrastructure needed
to achieve the preceding goals. Other major goals include the maintenance of the religious and moral values of Islam, as well as the internal security and national independence of the kingdom. These
goals are interrelated but not necessarily harmonious or mutually reinforcing. In the course of development, the authorities may be
obliged to trade gains in one direction for losses in another.

The development strategy described in the plan involves heavy
emphasis on investment in modern capital equipment in a massive effort to increase the output of the nonoil economy. This amounts to a
"big push" strategy, in which the nation's new oil wealth would be
utilized in simultaneous campaigns to develop and modernize all of
the major economic sectors.

The cumulative financial resources allocated to the plan are
$141.5 billion, more than $20,000 per capita. Major construction
projects account for 52 percent of the total; administration and national
security account for 23.4 percent; and foreign assistance and contin-
gencies account for 12.7 percent. On a program basis, emphasis is
placed on agricultural and water resource development and electrical-
generating capacity throughout the country, as well as a hydrocarbon-
based industrial complex centered in the Eastern Province. The latter
accounts for 10 percent of total planned outlays and provides for new
capacity in petroleum refining and gas collection, as well as in fertilizer, petrochemical, steel, and aluminum production.[15]

Factor imbalance, a basic feature of underdevelopment, represents a serious constraint on the successful implementation of this
Saudi plan. Saudi Arabia has enormous capital resources but severe
shortages of other productive factors, especially the human skills re-

quired to administer a development effort as massive and comprehensive as this. Expensive technical and managerial skills can be hired in the West, but middle- and lower-level supervisory personnel, as well as skilled and semiskilled manual workers, will have to be drawn from the surrounding Arab countries and the East.

With the other petroleum-exporting countries exerting similar development efforts, the aggregate effect is strong upward pressure on wage costs and, ultimately, on domestic price levels. Although the plan assumes an increase of 500,000 in the foreign work force by 1980, the increase needed to accomplish the plan could well be larger. Even so, an increase of 500,000 means that, by 1980, non-Saudis would account for at least 35 percent of the labor force in Saudi Arabia; in 1975, non-Saudis officially accounted for scarcely 20 percent of the labor force.* The implied influx will strain the fabric of the traditional Saudi society. It may be that Saudi Arabia's goal of rapid development will be at the expense of its goal of maintaining the moral values of its puritanical variant of Islam.

If the past is any guide to the future, the cash outlays prescribed by the Saudi plan point to continuous inflation. Government spending is the primary determinant of the money supply, and, to achieve the cumulative outlays envisioned in the plan, the government will have to increase its spending from the fiscal 1974 level at a compound rate of 30 percent per annum throughout the planning period. If the government's net domestic spending and the money supply were to grow at comparable rates, inflation would be unavoidable. Assuming that the plan's real growth target of 10.2 percent per annum is consistent with the economy's long-term growth potential and that the velocity of money spending remains constant, this combination of rates implies inflation of about 20 percent a year. But velocity is not likely to remain stable. Knowing that, according to the plan, spending will have to rise year by year, the public would learn to anticipate inflation and would tend to accelerate spending to dispose of cash before it suffered further losses of purchasing power. After a time, inflation becomes self-reinforcing. Rising inflationary expectations can lead to a rise in velocity and an acceleration in the rate of inflation, without an acceleration in the growth of government spending or the money supply.

Real factors also play a role in accelerating inflation. When infrastructure is rudimentary and supplies of domestic products are

---

*Considerable uncertainty surrounds the question of the size of the Saudi labor force and its composition. It is quite possible that non-Saudis already accounted for as much as half of the labor force by 1975.

relatively inelastic, rapid growth in government spending quickly leads to growth in aggregate demand, which cannot be satisfied by imports or domestic production. As the flow of imports becomes jammed in ports and internal distribution channels, industrial projects are stalled and completed projects are underutilized for want of the other necessary factors of production. Plans are disrupted, and real resources are wasted. Under these circumstances, the productivity of additional capital can quickly fall to zero. A massive disgorgement of funds can lead to inflation without commensurate real growth. For these reasons, the goal of the second Saudi plan may not be fully achieved. Administrative chaos and port congestion, as well as social and political tensions arising from inflation and mass immigration, are likely to force reductions in the rates of financial expansion and new development undertakings.

The Saudi case is more representative of conditions in Kuwait, Libya, Qatar, and the United Arab Emirates than in Iran, Iraq, or Algeria. The latter countries have greater capital absorptive potential, although they, too, are faced with shortages of strategic human resources and with deficient infrastructures. Differences are more a matter of degree than of kind.

In the end, the big push strategy seems inappropriate for the oil states of the Middle East, given their present stage of development. In Rostovian terms, the oil boom has propelled them into a drive for maturity without their ever having gone through the preconditions of growth stage. The oil states would be well advised to resist this temptation. Rather than trying to telescope 50 years of development into 5, a more selective approach, in which barriers at each stage of development are identified and reduced or eliminated in a more orderly fashion, would produce better long-term results. The danger of the inflationary big push is that, through it, less may be achieved in the long run than was possible at the outset.

The recent economic history of the Middle East contains numerous additional examples of the growth-inhibiting role of factor imbalance. Ironically, the development that might relieve factor shortages may be precluded by those very shortages.

Without the benefit of increasing petroleum revenue, the nonoil states have faced the perennial problems of capital and foreign exchange shortage. Egypt's planning experience demonstrates the constraint a dearth of foreign exchange can impose on a big push development effort.*

---

*Egypt is relatively well supplied with indigenous expertise and has employed the services of several outstanding foreign economists.

Egypt came close to the target rate of gross domestic product (GDP) growth during the period of the First Five-Year Plan. The growth rate of gross fixed-capital formation was virtually on target, and the ratio of gross investment of GDP was pushed to the 18 percent level. But as a consequence, imports outran exports, and international reserves were depleted. Adding to the increasing drain of resources was the Egyptian military intervention in the Yemen. Thus, the targeted level of investment could not be maintained, and the growth of real investment declined after 1964. Although credits were obtained from France, Japan, and Italy and a loan was provided by Kuwait, the foreign exchange difficulty worsened. In December 1966, Egypt was forced to default on repayments due the International Monetary Fund (IMF) and to retrench, adopting austerity measures and abandoning its Second Five-Year Plan. A three-year interim plan for 1967-70 was prepared but abandoned because of the 1967 War. In the mid 1970s, the economy continued to be run on a discretionary basis despite the preparation of a new ten-year plan in 1971.

Chronic inability to meet the savings required by investment targets has been a major deterrent to development among the nonoil states. Often, neither overall growth nor investment targets are achieved because of failure to generate the necessary domestic savings. Under these circumstances, the nonoil countries' dependence on external assistance and their foreign indebtedness grows.

Historically, planning in the Middle East has suffered from political interference and ideological bias. The cumulative burden of past errors, a lack of adequately evaluated projects, a lack of plan and budget coordination, and insufficient implementation machinery add to the difficulties. Most of these problems are connected, in one way or another, to the shortage of skills. The insufficiency of bureaucratic capabilities, in relation to tasks, leads to decisions that contribute to the needless disruption of economic life.

Public economic planning, like private economic planning, needs to be conducted in a predictable political environment. Political interference leads to wasteful decisions and inconsistent policies. Planning boards are subjected to frequent changes in composition and responsibility. At times, responsibility is limited to planning; at other

------

The First Five-Year Plan (1960-65) employed balance sheets of sources and uses of 300 commodities for the base and end years of the plan. A computer optimization model of an economy of ten decisional sectors was available for guiding the choices of the authorities (see Ragnar Frisch, How to Plan, Memorandum no. 102 [Cairo: Institute of National Planning, 1963]).

times, it is extended to include implementation as well. Planning responsibility may be limited to the public sector and then expanded to include the direction of the private sector also. Changes in cabinets within regimes, as well as in regimes themselves, lead to changes in the planning apparatus. The implication is that planning agencies are focal points for political rivalries, yet substantial political independence is a prerequisite to productive economic decisions.

Middle Eastern planning machinery frequently lacks adequate arrangements for the implementation of plans and the coordination of planning and budgeting. In the Maghreb states, plans have mentioned the need to coordinate the financial, material, and administrative aspects of programs without providing details.[16] Often, manpower training is not linked to industrial investment programs.[17] Political instability and rotating ministerial responsibilities also impede implementation. When prospective tenure is short and burdens of responsibility are shifted frequently, little serious implementation will be forthcoming. Personnel changes cause frequent amendments to programs, and projects are likely to be cancelled or delayed.[18]

Middle Eastern planners are sometimes pushed into hasty and wasteful programs. These may be undertaken in order to qualify for grants or loans from industrial countries and international development agencies. Wasteful programs may also result from sales pressure. Sales representatives of European, U.S., or Japanese firms are present in the area in increasing numbers, encouraging unwary clients to purchase finished products, machines, or even whole factories. Sales campaigns include ready-made feasibility studies showing high rates of return on invested capital. These may be based on dubious assumptions and faulty data.

Given the narrowness of domestic markets and the generally low labor productivity, one doubts that some heavy industrial projects are worth their cost. Although import substitution is certainly a defensible strategy, one questions whether high-cost domestic steel, for instance, is a proper item to substitute for a lower-cost foreign product. Algerian authorities have admitted that the new steel complex at Annaba, with capacity two times that of Algerian demand, will not be commercially viable, although it is justified by the assumption that it will provide externalities that will encourage the growth of ancillary industries.[19] Examples of equally dubious projects, often in the name of autarky, can be found in other countries of the Middle East. Against this sort of criticism must be weighed the counterargument that progress comes through "learning by doing." If developing nations postpone industrialization until they can match the mature economies in terms of efficiency, they will never begin industrialization.

Entrepreneurial and technical skills in both the public and private sectors are in short supply in most of the countries. Consequently, modernization is undertaken with an insufficient stock of modern skills, and to make matters worse, manpower training is frequently not coordinated with the needs of the economy.

Shortages of skills are worsened on occasion by the economic policies of the government. The nationalization of the larger firms in Socialist countries accelerated the migration of trained technical and managerial people. Even experienced bureaucrats have moved abroad because of the policy of making appointments to positions of power and influence on the basis of loyalty to the regime, rather than on the basis of training or ability. The allocation of status and responsibility on the basis of loyalty rather than ability appears to be a general characteristic of Middle Eastern bureaucracy. The emphasis on loyalty impedes the development of an efficient, politically neutral bureaucracy.

The particularly acute shortage of skilled labor raises the cost of projects and distorts the pattern of public sector development from that intended by planners. The scarcity of technical skills is reflected in the lack of local construction firms capable of undertaking modern industrial projects. In many cases, foreign contracting is unavoidable. Large projects attract foreign firms, and, in such cases, tenders may be invited on an international basis. Local firms, however, have to be relied upon for the construction of smaller projects. Consequently, smaller- and medium-sized projects have not been completed on schedule because of the dearth of local firms willing to undertake them. This problem exists in varying degrees throughout the area. The result is a distortion in the pattern of project implementation, with a bias toward the completion of large projects.

For their part, foreign firms and consultants are not always successful in the Middle East. Life in many parts of the area is harsh. Firms may find the lack of logistic and maintenance facilities a serious impediment, and costs often turn out to be higher than originally estimated. The advice of foreign consultants may be ignored, and the opportunity to exploit the services of foreign firms often is not fully utilized.

How effective is planning in the Middle East? In dealing with this issue, it should be recognized that no objective proof can be offered one way or the other. It is unlikely that any foreigner ever can be more than an observer of the decision-making process. Furthermore, no one is likely to be in a position of being a close observer of the planning process in all of the countries under consideration. For these reasons, judgment as to the efficacy of planning cannot be unequivocal. In the sense of having a direct impact on decisions governing the allocation of resources, however, planning in the Middle East may be judged as being ineffectual. Largely because of the absence of functioning implementation mechanisms, planning tends to be an exercise conducted in isolation.

This applies even to Egypt, the country best endowed with trained economists and engineers. According to observers close to the planning process, Egypt's elaborate decision model had no practical influence on Egyptian decision making.[20] Investment decisions in Egypt (1960-65) were not made according to plan criteria. According to Donald Mead, investment decisions were formed through a process of political bargaining among the ministries.[21] Egypt's First Five-Year Plan was a collection of investment projects that originated in the various ministries and then were incorporated into a single document. Although some ministries attempted to select projects on the basis of a comparison of rates of return on invested capital, the resulting investment program cannot be rated highly in terms of coordination or optimality.[22]

Another authority on Egyptian development, Patrick O'Brien, notes that when the minister of Planning attempted to hold projects within the limits of available resources, the ministers submitting project proposals usually succeeded in pushing their favored projects into the plan. The investment program that was fashioned in this way was not consistent with the available supplies of manpower, savings, and foreign exchange.[23]

Thus, by sifting the evidence of poor project evaluation, political interference, skill shortages, and the lack of implementation mechanisms, one is forced to the conclusion that planning, in general, has not been effective in the area. Bureaucratic decisions continue to be made on a traditional, political basis.

Available evidence suggests that inefficiency is a serious problem in those economies in which centralized, bureaucratic control has progressed the farthest—as in Egypt, where government-induced price distortions may account for more inefficiency in production than do the other mistakes and red tape of the bureaucracy.* Government-regulated prices encourage a pattern of production that is not in line with consumers' preferences. This misallocation is revealed by shortages, queues, and black markets.

---

*According to political analysts, only the Israeli bureaucracy may be judged as modern. The bureaucracies of Egypt, Lebanon, Libya, Morocco, Syria, Tunisia, and Turkey are rated as semimodern, that is, rationalized but of limited efficiency because of shortages of skilled personnel. Elsewhere, bureaucracies are classified as traditional or as postcolonial structures in the process of being reconstituted (see Arthur S. Banks and Robert B. Textor, A Cross Polity Survey, rev. ed. [1968][made available through the Inter-University Consortium for Political Research]).

Price determination in the public sector and the inefficiency of state economic enterprises have become sources of concern in the non-socialist economies. One source of difficulty has been the policy of setting prices below unit costs. The intent is to subsidize consumers, but the resulting welfare effects are mixed. Because of their losses, state firms can contribute little to their own capital formation; and public funds must be used for subsidies, which could have been used to advantage elsewhere. Increased efficiency would serve to keep prices low, while freeing public money for general welfare purposes.

It is unfortunate that ideas and attitudes concerning economic planning were formed in the Middle East in the 1950s or before, during the heyday of the cult of the plan. In the 1950s, central planning with priority on the expansion of heavy industry brought rapid growth to the Soviet Union. Consequently, central planning and centralized bureaucratic control of the economy were thought to be essential to socialist development. Public ownership of the means of production was seen as being inseparably combined with the central bureaucratic direction of the economy. In the 1960s, the East European states began to turn to decentralized decision making as a means of increasing efficiency. Under the pressure of increasing bottlenecks and delays, declining capital productivity, and flagging innovation, central authorities began to grant local plant managers greater autonomy in day-to-day operations, interfirm contracting, and so on. Profits, sales, and rates of return on investment also began to be used instead of quota fulfillment as success criteria for state firms. In the interest of flexibility and efficiency, decentralized decision making became a serious alternative.

One of the great lessons of modern economic development is that it may be desirable to separate formal ownership from the effective control of the means of production. What matters finally is not so much who owns property but, rather, how it is used and how its product is distributed. The recent experience of the European socialist states reflects a rediscovery of the market mechanism as a more efficient way of organizing production than central direction. The market is being used increasingly, while public ownership of the means of production is being retained.

The socialist states of the Middle East should benefit from following this example. A return to the profit motive and market guidance would encourage the production of things most needed in society. Genuine worker participation in the decision making of autonomous firms and shares in the profits of such firms would provide a more effective incentive system than the present one, in which wages bear little connection to productivity. The decentralization of decision making would lower the cost of bureaucratic ineptitude and red tape. Just as centralization of decision making tends to bureaucratize the entire economy, depriving it of any meaningful objective test of economic performance, decentralization would restore the beneficial guidance of the market. Extra income would accrue to firms and workers producing goods desired by society in the least costly way; losses would discourage production by wasteful methods, as well as the production of goods not needed by society. Decentralization would thus hasten the day when tariff barriers could be removed and exports increased through improved efficiency.

Reform in this direction would still leave an abundant challenge to the capabilities of government. The development of infrastructure and water resources, the provision of health and educational services, in addition to the conduct of international affairs and the maintenance of justice and order, imply tasks sufficient to tax the capacities of all Middle Eastern governments. In addition, the government would still be in a position to regulate the aggregate division of resources between consumption and capital goods production, but the detailed composition of production could be left to the market.

Among the Middle Eastern socialist states, the problem of bureaucracy is crucial. Economic alternatives to bureaucratic control are available; whether a move toward decentralization is politically feasible is another matter. Once power is centralized, those who hold it can be expected to resist reforms that would tend to dilute it.

NOTES

1. Charles Issawi, Egypt at Mid-Century (London: Oxford University Press, 1954), p. 126.

2. Doreen Warriner, Land Reform in Principle and Practice (Oxford: Clarendon Press, 1969), p. 90.

3. Jacques Berque, "The Rural System of the Maghrib," in State and Society in Independent North Africa, ed. L. C. Brown (Washington, D.C.: Middle East Institute, 1966), p. 200.

4. Adel Kamal, "Feudalism and Land Reform," in The Middle East: A Handbook, ed. Michael Adams (New York: Praeger, 1971), p. 495.

5. Food and Agricultural Organization of the United Nations, Production Yearbook (various issues).

6. The International Bank for Reconstruction and Development, The Economic Development of Syria (Baltimore: Johns Hopkins University Press, 1955), p. 19.

7. United Nations Economic and Social Office in Beirut, "Development Planning and Social Objectives in Syria," Studies on Selected Development Problems in Various Countries in the Middle East, 1971 (New York: United Nations, 1971), p. 6.

8. Kamal, op. cit., p. 498.

9. United Nations Economic and Social Office in Beirut, "Past Developments and Growth Prospects in the Agricultural Sector of Syria," Studies on Selected Development Problems in Various Countries in the Middle East, 1971 (New York: United Nations, 1971), p. 36.

10. Ibid.

11. A. K. S. Lambton, The Persian Land Reform: 1962-1966 (Oxford: Clarendon Press, 1969), pp. 1-30.

12. Ibid., p. 63.

13. For a discussion of modernization as a historical process of change, see C. E. Black, The Dynamics of Modernization (New York: Harper & Row, 1966), p. 7.

14. For an elaboration, see Raymond Vernon, "Comprehensive Model-Building in the Planning Process: The Case of the Less Developed Economies," Economic Journal 76, no. 301 (March 1966): 57-69.

15. These data are drawn from United States-Saudi Arabia Joint Commission on Economic Cooperation, Summary of Saudi Arabian Five Year Development Plan 1975-1980 (Washington, D.C.: Department of the Treasury, 1975).

16. Economic Commission for Africa, Economic Survey of Africa 2, North Africa Sub-Region (New York: United Nations, 1968), p. 126.

17. Ibid.

18. For a survey of Iraqi planning problems in the 1960s, see United Nations Economic and Social Office in Beirut, "Plan Implementation in Iraq," Studies on Selected Development Problems in Various Countries in the Middle East, 1969 (New York: United Nations, 1969), pp. 1-17.

19. Quarterly Economic Review: Algeria and Morocco, no. 2 (London: Economist Intelligence Unit, 1969), p. 7.

20. Bent Hansen and Girgis A. Marzouk, Development and Economic Policy in the UAR (Amsterdam: North-Holland, 1965), p. 307.

21. Donald C. Mead, Growth and Structural Change in the Egyptian Economy (Homewood, Ill.: R. D. Irwin, 1967), p. 107.

22. Hansen and Marzouk, op. cit., pp. 286-94.

23. Patrick O'Brien, Revolution in Egypt's Economic System (London: Oxford University Press, 1966), pp. 158-59.

4

FINANCE

Policy differences between the mature economies and those of the Third World are largely the result of priority and emphasis. Industrialized countries tend to be more concerned with levels of employment, price stability, and external payments equilibrium; developing countries may give higher priority to such nation-building goals as new lines of production, improved administration, additional infrastructure, and the provision of welfare services. Regardless of where emphasis is placed, modern governments everywhere employ budgetary policy in pursuit of selected objectives. The budget is, in practice, the most important strategic instrument available to the state.

REVENUES AND EXPENDITURES

Modern governments obtain command over resources through taxation, the sale of goods and services, the sale of securities locally or abroad, the solicitation of foreign aid in the form of transfers, and the creation of money. In practice, the particular mix of sources employed reflects an individual country's unique circumstances, for example, its per capita income level, its prevailing ideology, its class structure, its ability to export, and its foreign alliances.

The share of government revenue collected from direct personal taxes and indirect business taxes is relatively small in the typical oil state. As one would expect, oil revenue collected from government or foreign production units accounts for the preponderance of current revenue in these countries, and the contribution of this source has been of increasing relative importance. (See Table 4.1.)

TABLE 4.1

Sources of Government Revenue, Middle Eastern Countries,
1967 and 1973

Country	Wealth and Income Taxes[a]		Indirect Taxes[b]		Royalties, Rents, and Enterprise Income[c]	
	1967	1973	1967	1973	1967	1973
Major oil states						
Algeria	22.5[d]	14.2	42.2[d]	34.4	35.3[d]	51.1
Iran	10.6	12.2	25.9	19.8	63.5	68.0
Iraq	7.5	6.3	16.4	12.4	76.1	81.3
Kuwait	0.2[d]	0.0	2.1[d]	1.3	97.7[d]	98.7
Libya	7.9	5.1	10.5	11.4	81.6	83.5
Saudi Arabia	10.7	0.2	5.0	3.1	84.3	96.7
Other states						
Egypt	25.8	32.3	45.1	58.7	29.1	9.0
Israel	44.0	33.1	32.7	41.3	23.3	25.6
Jordan	15.6	13.2	48.2	45.6	36.2	41.2
Lebanon	20.7	16.7	45.2	43.3	34.1	40.0
Morocco	28.0	28.1	45.4	55.9	26.6	16.0
Northern Yemen	15.9	11.4	66.6	68.1	17.5	20.5
Sudan	5.5	11.9	50.4	54.2	44.1	33.9
Syria	21.5	18.7	19.9	20.8	58.6	60.5
Tunisia	28.2	29.5	45.0	43.5	26.8	27.0
Turkey	34.0	41.7	38.4	41.0	27.6	17.3

[a]Includes income, property, inheritance, and livestock taxes.
Oil revenues are excluded.
[b]Includes mostly sales taxes and customs duties.
[c]Includes oil revenue, as well as other rents, royalties, and
receipts from government enterprises.
[d]Refers to 1968.

Source: International Bank for Reconstruction and Development, World Tables (1975).

In the Middle East, indirect taxes are typically the main source of government revenue among states without major petroleum resources. As in the developing countries generally, there is, necessarily, a heavy reliance on indirect taxation. When populations are comprised largely of peasant farmers and small suq merchants, the revenue return from direct taxes may not be worth their collection costs. A tax on personal income is effective only when the distribution structure shows the presence of a substantial middle-income class. In the absence of such a class, a personal income tax tends to be an easily evaded levy on the rich. Under these conditions, direct taxes are unproductive in terms of revenue unless backed by unusual moral force, as in the case of the zakat.* Furthermore, when record keeping is not widespread and much production never enters organized markets, the estimation of income in terms of the unit of account and the determination of appropriate tax rates may prove to be formidable analytical problems. Although these difficulties also pertain in some degree to indirect taxes, these are at least easier to administer because of the relatively small number of modern sector traders and importers.

Regardless of the method of taxation, both the ordinary revenues and the total expenditures of government have, in recent years, tended to rise relative to GDP. (See Table 4.2.) Among the oil states, the petroleum price increases of 1973 greatly increased government revenue. Meanwhile, throughout the region, military requirements, rapid population growth, and increasing urbanization combine to increase the expenditure commitments of the governments.

Certain oil states, notably Saudi Arabia and Kuwait, have been unable to keep spending abreast of receipts. Gauged in terms of outlays relative to revenues, their budgetary surpluses increased sharply in the mid-1970s. Elsewhere, budgetary deficits continue to be a problem, and especially so among the Arab-Israeli confrontation states. Consolidated spending on current and capital accounts far

---

*The zakat was a wealth tax usually assessed at the rate of 2.5 percent on gold and silver, cattle, grain, and merchandise. Originally prescribed by the Koran as voluntary alms, the zakat evolved into an obligatory wealth tax, which was used by the state to aid the poor, to build mosques, and for general expenditures. In the Abbasid period, the heyday of the Arab Empire, the zakat was extended to include land and other tangible assets. Although there is evidence of widespread evasion in late Abbasid times, the successful use of this tax in early Islam shows that direct taxation was feasible when imposed as a moral imperative.

TABLE 4.2

Some Dimensions of Public Finance, Middle Eastern Countries, 1970s
(percent)

Country	Revenues as a Percent of GDP		Outlays as a Percent of GDP		Outlays Relative to Revenues	
	1970-72	1973-75	1970-72	1973-75	1970-72	1973-75
Major oil states						
Algeria	31	44	37	50	119	114
Iran	24	39	28	35	117	90
Iraq	30	37*	31	40*	103	108*
Kuwait	34	62	27	22	79	35
Libya	46	26*	32	30*	70	115*
Saudi Arabia	36	51	30	23	83	45
Other states						
Egypt	20	29	32	45	160	155
Israel	38	41	51	72	134	176
Jordan	15	20	38	48	253	240
Lebanon	16	14*	17	20*	106	143*
Morocco	19	25	23	30	121	120
Sudan	23	22*	25	26*	109	118*
Syria	23	27	31	45	135	167
Tunisia	23	23*	26	28*	113	122*
Turkey	20	19	22	22	110	116

*Refers to 1973 only.

Note: Figures are means of annual ratios.

Sources: Estimates are based on data found in International Bank for Reconstruction and Development, World Tables (1975); International Monetary Fund, International Financial Statistics; and miscellaneous country sources.

exceeds ordinary revenues; thus, foreign and domestic indebtedness and demands for external grant assistance continue to grow. Military emphasis raises the states' shares of total spending to unusually high levels, irrespective of the ideological biases of the individual state involved.

THE PROBLEM OF MILITARY SPENDING

Regional development in the Middle East is retarded by the area's high propensity for military spending.* Obviously, military outlays absorb resources that could otherwise be used for civilian consumption, capital formation, or loans to others for development purposes. Military spending is relatively high for several reasons.

Absence of constitutional restraints on the use of force and lack of mechanisms for the peaceful transfer of power contribute to unstable rule. [1] Muslim rulers have been replaced, more often than not, through violence. Under these circumstances, the first priority of a regime is its self-preservation; thus, forces sufficient to maintain internal security account for some basic level of military expenditure. Since the army is necessarily the guarantor of regimes, the army tends to become the regime and, in recent years, has played either an interventionist or a key supportive role in the political process of almost every Middle Eastern country.

Modern military capability requires more than military hardware; literate manpower and efficient logistic, communications, and maintenance systems are also necessary factors. Adequacy in these areas is mainly a function of the stage of development of the economy at large, and, for this reason if for no other, both military republics and conservative monarchies of the Middle East are striving for economic growth and structural change. Ironically, development may add to internal tensions.

Economic progress implies new skill requirements, with alterations in the structure of employment and the distribution of income. Urbanization and growing industrial employment mean a weakening of the traditional social structure and the values of the extended family. Those who are made worse off by these changes may become embit-

---

*According to data provided by the U.S. Arms Control and Disarmament Agency, the Middle Eastern region's incremental propensity for military spending (change in constant dollar military spending divided by change in constant dollar GNP) for the years 1966-75 was 0.16. For the Third World as a whole, the ratio was only 0.07.

tered and alienated, the raw material of social unrest. Those who gain may add to the tension by pushing for still more economic and political power.[2] When social change is rapid, unrest and discord are almost certain to follow, as in Syria, where the frequency of riots, demonstrations, and deaths by domestic violence increased sharply in the years of widespread nationalization and extension of government control.*

Ideological differences are a further source of tension that threaten internal security in many of the states of the area. Islamic conservatism, bourgeois reformism, and radical socialism are opposing social philosophies that find adherents in the countries of the Middle East. Pan-Arabism, the movement to establish a unified Arab state, is in conflict with a more narrowly defined, conventional nationalism in the area. Class, ethnic, and religious divisions also contribute to internal tensions.†

Internal considerations alone imply substantial military shares in the national budgets of the Middle East. But the preponderance of military spending is in response to international tensions. The Gulf area with its petroleum riches is of increasing world importance, and Iran's drive to fill the power vacuum left by the withdrawal of the British, as well as the threat of conquest by outside forces, has stimulated military spending in Saudi Arabia and Iraq. Given the growth of oil revenue in the 1970s, these major Gulf states have the resources to provide for inordinately large stocks of both offensive and defensive military equipment.

---

*In the period 1948-67, Syria experienced 54 protest demonstrations, 82 riots, and 1,800 deaths from domestic violence. During the years of extensive nationalization (1963-65), 43 percent of the demonstrations, 30 percent of the riots, and 60 percent of the deaths occurred. See C. L. Taylor and Michael C. Hudson, World Handbook of Political and Social Indicators, 2d ed. (New Haven, Conn.: Yale University Press, 1972), pp. 88, 96, 112.

†There is the ancient hostility between the desert and the town, that is, between the settled population and nomadic herdsmen. There are rebellious ethnic minority groups, such as the Kurdish nationalists in Iraq and blacks in southern Sudan, which have threatened internal security. The maldistribution of income, wealth, and economic opportunity in Lebanon contributed to the civil war and to the political disintegration there. Concerning religious diversity, Islam is not homogeneous, and there are numerous variant groups in the area. More significant as a potential source of instability is the tension between Muslims and non-Muslims—especially the tensions between Christians and Muslims in Lebanon and Egypt.

TABLE 4.3

Military Burden, Middle Eastern Countries, 1973-75

| Country | Per Capita Public Expenditures, 1973 (current U.S. dollars) | | | Military Expenditures | | | |
	Health	Education	Military	Millions of current U.S. dollars 1975	Percent of GNP 1973	1974	1975
Major oil states							
Algeria	8	46	9	302	1.7	2.3	2.5
Iran	8	28	73	7,760	9.6	13.6	14.9
Iraq	6	27	79	1,850	10.7	23.0	14.8
Kuwait	105	238	150	235	2.2	1.3	2.2
Libya	59	186	46	201	3.1	3.5	1.8
Oman	—	—	156	655	33.4	28.6	36.6
Qatar	—	—	133	106	4.0	2.8	7.0
Saudi Arabia	22	83	204	1,750	7.2	4.6	5.8
United Arab Emirates	—	—	69	59	1.0	0.6	0.8
Other states							
Egypt	6	11	48	1,340	15.5	15.4	11.7
Israel	16	110	1,137	4,160	41.0	30.5	34.6
Jordan	4	9	54	144	14.4	11.9	10.4
Lebanon	6	25	30	136*	2.4	3.4*	3.4*
Morocco	5	19	10	253	3.5	2.7	3.1
North Yemen	2	1	4	52	4.4	5.3	6.8
South Yemen	2	7	19	37	10.0	10.5	9.4
Sudan	1	6	6	121	3.7	3.2	2.6
Syria	2	14	56	837	15.5	11.1	16.8
Tunisia	10	28	7	65	1.4	1.4	1.6
Turkey	7	16	23	1,600	4.0	3.8	4.5

*Tentative estimate.

Sources: Ruth L. Sivard, World Military and Social Expenditures, 1976 (Leesburg, Va.: World Military and Social Expenditures Publications, 1976); and U.S., Arms Control and Disarmament Agency, World Military Expenditures and Arms Transfers 1966-1975 (Washington. D.C.: U.S. Arms Control and Disarmament Agency, 1976),

Paramount among sources of Middle Eastern tension, however, is the continuing Arab-Israeli dispute, which has dominated the politics of the area for more than a quarter of a century. The periodic Arab-Israeli wars are more accurately major battles in the unresolved struggle for control of Palestine. As a consequence of this protracted conflict, Israel and the surrounding Arab states are among the most militarily overburdened in the world. The extend of this problem can be gauged by comparing military spending as a percent of GNP in these countries with the world's rate of only about 6 percent. (See Table 4.3.)

In most of the countries of the Middle East, returns to human investment are high, so that forgone health and education programs are major elements in the opportunity cost of military spending. Per capita expenditures on public health, education, and military preparation therefore provide an indication of official priorities. Military development in the mid-1970s took precedence over human investment by wide margins in the Arab-Israeli confrontation states and around the Gulf. In these areas, per capita military spending was two to ten times greater than were expenditures for education; and in several cases, it was as much as 70 times greater than spending for public health. Conversely, in countries situated at a greater distance from these centers of tension, priorities were very different. The Maghreb states, as an illustration, spent much more per capita on educational than on military goals.

In terms of constant dollars, all-purpose military spending has accelerated in the two major areas of arms accumulation. In Saudi Arabia and Iran, real outlays rose fivefold between 1970 and 1975; in Iraq, they rose approximately threefold. Real spending for military purposes more than doubled in Israel in 1973, and substantial increases also occurred among the Arab belligerents.

The Middle Eastern arms trade reflects the patterns of the Cold War political alignments: Communist states have supplied Iraq, Egypt, and Syria; the United States and other Western exporters of arms have supplied Iran, Israel, and Turkey. Arms to other states have been more thinly spread in accordance with the regional strategies of the major suppliers. (See Table 4.4.) During the period 1965-74, the area absorbed over $20 billion worth of arms from outside sources. Of this total, the preponderance came from the United States (47 percent), followed by the USSR (34 percent). Progress toward restricting the traffic will depend on agreement between these two chief suppliers.

Without an equitable solution to the Palestine problem, the militarily overburdened confrontation states face the prospects of mounting foreign indebtedness and dependence on foreign suppliers of military grant aid. Their military requirements preclude the satisfaction of basic civilian needs and represent the major source of fiscal disorder.

TABLE 4.4

Cumulative Arms Transfers to Middle Eastern Countries from Major
Suppliers, 1965-74
(millions of current U.S. dollars)

| Country | Non-Communist | | Communist | | |
	United States	Other	USSR	Other	Total
Major oil states					
Algeria	3	8	248	37	296
Iran	2,702	471	589	115	3,877
Iraq	2	337	1,343	139	1,821
Kuwait	14	65	—	18	97
Libya	66	546	425	79	1,116
Oman	3	64	—	—	67
Qatar	—	2	—	—	2
Saudi Arabia	473	555	—	10	1,038
United Arab Emi- rates	—	77	—	—	77
Other states					
Egypt	—	138	2,465	177	2,780
Israel	3,856	171	—	4	4,031
Jordan	400	138	—	—	538
Lebanon	21	97	4	4	126
Morocco	52	69	9	29	159
North Yemen	1	37	27	—	65
South Yemen	—	12	114	—	126
Sudan	2	20	65	12	99
Syria	3	34	1,758	110	1,905
Tunisia	36	16	—	2	54
Turkey	2,017	131	—	154	2,302

Source: U.S., Arms Control and Disarmament Agency, World
Military Expenditures and Arms Transfers 1966-1975 (Washington,
D.C.: U.S. Arms Control and Disarmament Agency, 1976).

INTERNATIONAL ASSISTANCE

Basic development strategy in the Middle East necessarily involves fundamental improvements in factor proportions in order to relieve shortages and remove bottlenecks in the production process. Growth in a nation's infrastructure should parallel a campaign to enlarge the stock of fixed industrial equipment, and foreign assistance can provide the necessary supplement to domestic savings for these purposes. Military assistance may serve these ends indirectly when it frees domestic resources for civilian purposes. With the increasing role of government in economic decision making and with the growth in military spending have come the increasing dependence of the nonoil states on external sources of finance. Since 1967, current foreign payments deficits have increased relative to GDP among these countries. (See Table 4.5.)

Foreign assistance may be in the form of outright grants (transfers) or in the form of loans at concessional terms. As foreign debt service represents a long-term flow of resources from the debtor to the creditor country, the latter form of assistance implies economic costs, as well as benefits, for the aid recipient. When a country borrows beyond its debt service capacity, which depends on its productivity and ability to export, it risks its national integrity and political sovereignty, as the nineteenth-century experiences of Turkey, Egypt, and other Middle Eastern countries demonstrate. Economic assistance has other important political aspects as well. Aid programs may be designed to stimulate or dampen social change or to shore up a tottering friendly government. As the terms of assistance are negotiable, they are susceptible to the inclusion of political, as well as economic, costs and benefits.

The pattern of economic assistance to the Middle East in recent years clearly reflects the competition for clients by the major powers. Countries of strategic importance, such as Algeria and Turkey, have been able to attract substantial amounts of assistance from both the Western industrial states and Communist states. Others benefit from special relationships with the aid-supplying nations. In the data, Western aid totals are net disbursements, while Communist assistance is in the form of gross commitments, so that the levels of assistance recorded in Table 4.6 are not strictly comparable. Despite this accounting difference, it is possible to draw some inferences concerning aid trends and priorities.

Communist economic assistance tends to be more selective than Western support and to be concentrated on the politically more radical states. Western aid is more broadly spread, and it tends to be more consistently delivered through time. Reflecting the decline of Soviet influence after the October War, Communist aid to the region

TABLE 4.5

Foreign Payments Deficits, Middle Eastern Countries,
1967, 1973, 1974, and 1975

Country	Payments Deficits (-) as a Percent of GDP			
	1967	1973	1974	1975
Major oil states				
Algeria	-2.6	-11.5	2.1	-16.0
Iran	-1.7	0.3	26.5	10.2
Iraq	2.3	14.4	22.4	13.9
Kuwait	23.6	28.7	46.4	66.2
Libya	7.6	3.6	25.1	-2.0
Saudi Arabia	3.1	19.5	77.6	46.7
Other states				
Egypt	-5.2	-6.0	-13.5	-21.0
Israel	-16.0	-28.7	-35.8	-37.0
Jordan	-14.3	-22.7	-24.1	-34.3
Morocco	-3.9	-3.0	-1.6	-14.6
Sudan	-3.1	1.0	-8.6	-10.3
Syria	-2.7	-2.5	-7.5	-12.8
Tunisia	-13.3	-7.3	-6.6	-8.7
Turkey	-1.6	-3.1	-7.3	-9.6

Note: Transfers are excluded from current accounts.

Sources: International Monetary Fund, International Financial
Statistics (Washington, D.C.); and miscellaneous country data

in 1974 was far below the average of earlier years; aid to Syria alone
accounted for 95 percent of Communist aid to the region in 1974. At
the same time, Western assistance to the region at large increased,
as political and economic cooperation in the non-Communist world expanded to deal with the new power relationships that were emerging.
The increase in Western aid to Egypt was especially large in 1974,
reflecting a response to President Sadat's attempt to open the Egyptian
economy to foreign investment and world market forces.

As indicated by per capita income, there is little evidence that
economic need plays much of a role in determining the pattern of eco-

TABLE 4.6

Bilateral Official Economic Assistance to the Middle East, 1970–74
(current U.S. dollars)

Country	Net Bilateral Receipts from DAC Members[a]				Communist Economic Credits and Grants Extended[b]			
	Average, 1970–73 (millions of dollars)	1974	Per Capita, 1970–74[c]	Per Capita Rank	Average, 1970–73 (millions of dollars)	1974	Per Capita, 1970–74[c]	Per Capita Rank
Major oil states								
Algeria	97.9	100.7	34.54	4	137.8	—	38.64	4
Iran	2.8	1.4	0.40	18	88.8	—	11.39	6
Iraq	0.5	0.4	0.22	20	142.3	—	56.50	2
Kuwait	0.1	0.1	0.39	19	—	—	—	—
Libya	5.2	10.4	14.91	7	—	—	—	—
Oman	0.1	0.5	1.34	16	—	—	—	—
Saudi Arabia	0.4	1.3	0.57	17	—	—	—	—
United Arab Emirates	0.2	0.1	3.57	13	—	—	—	—
Other states								
Bahrain	0.4	0.7	10.27	9	—	—	—	—
Egypt	17.2	105.9	5.01	12	142.3	—	16.33	5

Israel	100.9	115.1	168.35	1	—	—	—	—
Jordan	60.9	64.8	125.31	2	—	—	—	—
Lebanon	6.0	5.4	10.22	10	—	9.0	3.12	10
Morocco	88.8	81.9	28.16	5	11.0	—	2.83	11
Northern Yemen	10.1	27.4	11.21	8	5.8	5.0	4.62	9
Southern Yemen	2.0	5.0	8.50	11	16.3	—	43.05	3
Sudan	6.2	33.2	3.50	14	41.8	—	10.07	7
Syria	1.2	5.5	1.53	15	103.5	285.0	103.93	1
Tunisia	101.6	123.8	99.30	3	10.0	—	7.49	8
Turkey	152.6	27.9	17.24	6	42.8	—	4.62	9
Total	655.1	715.5	16.94	—	742.0	299.0	17.30	—

[a]Includes grants and loans at concessional terms from the Development Assistance Committee (DAC) of the Organization for Economic Cooperation and Development. Members are Australia, Austria, Belgium, Canada, Denmark, Finland, France, West Germany, Italy, Japan, the Netherlands, New Zealand, Norway, Sweden, Switzerland, the United Kingdom, the United States, and the Commission of the European Economic Committee.

[b]Communist donors include Bulgaria, China, Czechoslovakia, East Germany, Hungary, Poland, Romania, and the USSR.

[c]Total receipts for 1970 through 1974 divided by the population estimate for 1972.

Sources: Organization for Economic Cooperation and Development, Development Cooperation Review 1975 (Paris: OECD, 1975); and U.S. Department of State, Communist States and Developing Countries: Aid and Trade in 1974, Special Report no. 23 (Washington, D.C.: Department of State, February 1976).

nomic assistance.* It seems probable that a state's place in the rank order of per capita assistance depends more on the donor's strategic considerations than on its level of poverty or stage of development.

The new era of high-priced oil marks the appearance of a third major source of international economic assistance. Since 1961, Kuwait Fund for Arab Economic Development has been an important source of capital, and following the precipitous rise in oil prices, several other oil states established similar outlets.† In 1974, the first full year following the main price increases, the petroleum exporters committed $3.8 billion in concessional aid, plus a nonconcessional commitment of $3.2 billion, for a total resource commitment of $7 billion. (See Table 4.7.) In 1975, the total resource commitment of the major oil states rose to nearly $8.3 billion. Although net disbursements lagged behind commitments, there was evidence of some improvement in delivery, as net disbursements reached 65 percent of commitments in 1975, up from 59 percent in 1974.

The financial conditions offered by the Middle Eastern aid suppliers vary widely in terms of rigor. Among the more radical states—Algeria, Iraq, and Libya—90 percent or more of concessional assistance was in the form of direct grants. For the Arab Gulf states, 70 to 80 percent were grants; but in Iran, only 32 percent were grants. For a comparison of these terms with those of other suppliers, the overall grant element in the total official development assistance of the major industrial countries—Development Assistance Committee (DAC) of the Organization for Economic Cooperation and Development (OECD)—was 89 percent in 1975.

Given the region's development needs, it is to be expected that assistance provided by the petroleum exporters will be more geo-

---

*For instance, during the period 1970-74, Israel received $168 of bilateral assistance per capita from Western sources, while the Sudan received $3.50 per capita; yet Israel's per capita income was nearly 25 times larger. During the period, Iraq's allocation of per capita assistance from Communist sources was over 12 times larger than Northern Yemen's, while the former's income per capita was at least 8 times greater.

†In the mid-1970s, these included the Special Arab Fund for Africa, the Organization of Arab Petroleum Exporting Countries (OAPEC) Special Account, the Arab Monetary Fund, the Arab Fund for Economic and Social Development Bank, the Arab Bank for Economic Development in Africa, the Organization of Petroleum Exporting Countries (OPEC) Special Fund, and the Gulf Organization for Development in Egypt.

TABLE 4.7

Major Middle Eastern Oil States as Suppliers of Resources for Development, 1974 and 1975
(millions of current U.S. dollars)

Item	Algeria	Iran	Iraq	Kuwait	Libya	Qatar	Saudi Arabia	United Arab Emirates	Total
Concessional aid commitments									
1974	60.7	799.7	492.6	494.8	235.8	128.1	1,012.9	541.8	3,766.4
1975	34.5	1,272.3	320.6	612.7	132.4	203.2	1,676.3	399.4	4,651.4
Nonconcessional commitments									
1974	—	534.0	75.0	394.0	256.5	134.2	1,515.5	334.9	3,244.1
1975	11.7	364.0	—	1,768.8	283.0	0.3	788.3	383.1	3,599.2
Total commitments									
1974	60.7	1,333.7	567.6	888.8	492.3	262.3	2,528.4	876.7	7,010.5
1975	46.2	1,636.3	320.6	2,381.5	415.4	203.5	2,464.6	782.5	8,250.6
Net disbursements									
1974	43.0	664.5	411.6	612.3	249.1	121.1	1,498.7	520.9	4,121.2
1975	28.4	721.4	249.6	1,147.2	358.7	180.2	2,014.5	642.9	5,342.9
Net disbursements as a percent of commitments									
1974	71.0	50.0	73.0	69.0	51.0	46.0	59.0	59.0	59.0
1975	61.0	44.0	78.0	48.0	86.0	89.0	82.0	82.0	65.0
Net disbursements of concessional assistance as a percent of GNP									
1974	0.4	0.7	3.1	2.2	1.0	4.3	2.5	3.9	
1975	0.1	0.9	1.5	2.8	1.6	6.4	2.6	4.6	

Note: Contributions to the IMF oil facility are excluded.

Source: Organization for Economic Cooperation and Development, Development Cooperation Review 1976 (Paris: OECD, 1976).

TABLE 4.8

Direction of Concessional Commitments by the Major Middle Eastern
Oil States, 1974 and 1975

Bilateral Commitments	1974 Millions of current U.S. Dollars	1974 Percent	1975 Millions of current U.S. Dollars	1975 Percent
Middle East	1,743.0	46.3	2,363.4	50.8
Bahrain	19.2	0.5	4.7	0.1
Egypt	675.5	17.9	985.5	21.2
Jordan	192.3	5.1	267.5	5.8
Lebanon	107.8	2.9	—	—
Morocco	49.2	1.3	87.4	1.9
Oman	150.6	4.0	148.9	3.2
North Yemen	90.2	2.3	94.1	2.0
South Yemen	28.5	0.8	50.2	1.1
Sudan	54.4	1.4	90.5	1.9
Syria	303.3	8.1	501.5	10.8
Tunisia	66.2	1.8	71.4	1.5
Turkey	—	—	31.9	0.7
Other	5.8	0.2	29.8	0.6
Africa	201.8	5.4	263.5	5.7
Asia	1,149.7	30.5	1,446.5	31.1
All others	11.3	0.3	6.0	0.1
Total	3,105.8	82.5	4,079.4	87.7
Commitments to multilateral organizations	660.6	17.5	572.0	12.3
Total concessional commitments	3,766.4	100.0	4,651.4	100.0

Source: Organization for Economic Cooperation and Development, Development Cooperation Review, 1976 (Paris: OECD, 1976).

graphically concentrated than that provided by the great powers. (See Table 4.8.) At mid-decade, other Middle Eastern countries received about 50 percent of the oil states' concessional commitments, and the Asian states, particularly India, received 30 percent. Among Middle Eastern countries, the shares of the confrontation states (Egypt, Syria, and Jordan) accounted for nearly 40 percent of the total concessional commitments of oil states in 1975. Although Africa's share was initially quite modest, it will surely be larger in the later 1970s. At the first Afro-Arab summit conference, held in Cairo in 1977, Saudi Arabia alone committed $1 billion to African economic development; and, as other petroleum exporters also increased their pledges, Arab commitments approached the $2 billion assistance goal then sought by the African nations.

At mid-decade, development assistance from within the region was far in excess of official aid flowing to the Middle East from external sources. Aside from the Arab Gulf states' aid, it is unlikely that internally generated assistance will continue to flow indefinitely at these high levels. Most of the petroleum exporters' current payments surpluses will probably decline as their capital absorptive capacities improve, so that funds available for export will diminish in the years ahead. Although transitory in nature, these funds are a boon to the area; and increasing emphasis on projects, as opposed to general support, indicates a definite focus on regional development. The share for projects in bilateral assistance from the petroleum exporters rose from about 33 percent in 1974 to about 60 percent in 1975.

On balance, the petroleum-exporting countries have responded generously to the aid-giving potentialities of their sudden affluence. Among the Arab petroleum exporters of the Gulf, concessional aid disbursements as a fraction of GNP range from 2.5 percent to more than 6 percent, and, as a group, the oil states of the Middle East provided assistance amounting to nearly 2 percent of GNP in 1975. This compares favorably to the aid-giving performance of industrial countries. In 1975, official development disbursements of DAC countries amounted to only 0.36 percent of combined GNP.

MONEY, PRICES, AND THE PUBLIC DEBT

Borrowing abroad has appeal in the Third World at large because it permits capital formation to go forward at a faster rate than it could through reliance on domestic savings alone. The evidence at hand indicates that, aside from the Arab oil states of the Gulf, foreign indebtedness relative to the value of production is substantial. (See Table 4.9.)

TABLE 4.9

Relative Size and Cost of Externally Held Public Debt, Middle
Eastern Countries, 1967 and 1974
(percent)

Country	Disbursed External Public Debt Relative to GNP		Foreign Debt Service Cost Relative to Merchandise Exports	
	1967	1974	1967	1974
Major oil states				
Algeria	15	36	7	18
Iran	9	13	5	6
Iraq	10	3	1	1
Kuwait	—	—	—	—
Libya	—	—	—	—
Saudi Arabia	—	—	—	—
Other states				
Egypt	25	19	28	23
Israel	34	48	25	33
Jordan	13	26	5	16
Lebanon	2	4	1	8
Morocco	18	16	10	8
Sudan	13	10	6	15
Syria	14	10	19	7
Tunisia	38	27	32	10
Turkey	12	12	20	15

Sources: International Bank for Reconstruction and Development, World Tables (1975); and Organization for Economic Cooperation and Development, Development Cooperation Review 1976 (Paris: OECD, 1976).

External borrowing, however, implies costs as well as benefits. Interest and amortization payments normally have to be made, and these imply real burdens for future generations. Other things being equal, the greater a country's capacity to export, the less will be the burden of a given level of debt service costs, so that the ratio of service costs to current exports is a good indication of the real burden of external debt. By this measure, several nonoil states, including the confrontation states, bear heavy external debt burdens. In contrast, among the oil states, only Algeria bears a real debt burden of much consequence.

Accurate and complete figures on the size and distribution of total government debt of the various states are not available. Nonetheless, it is reasonable to assume that, in most cases, securities in the hands of the nonbank public represent a relatively small share of total public debt (outstanding). Bond markets generally are not highly developed, so that the holdings of domestic banks or foreigners must account for most of the debt that is outstanding.

In the Middle East, central banks perform most of the traditional functions, such as serving as the government's fiscal agent, managing foreign exchange reserves, and supervising deposit money banks. * Nominal money is created primarily by government spending and, to a lesser extent, through the creation of excess reserves in deposit money banks, which leads to additional lending. The usual policy tools are changes in the reserve ratios required of deposit money banks and discount rate changes. Increasing reliance on banking institutions in the Middle East is indicated by the decline in the ratio of currency to the money supply (currency in the hands of the public plus bank demand deposits). In 1970, the currency ratio was more than 60 percent in most of the countries. By 1975, ratios exceeded 60 percent only in Iraq, Egypt, and Jordan.

Among the major oil states, the money supply grows when the authorities make new outlays of funds obtained through the conversion of export-earned foreign exchange into domestic currency. Among the nonoil states, a similar expansive effect occurs when the government sells bonds to the central bank and spends the proceeds. In both cases, the money supply grows by the amount of the new outlays. As some of the new currency will find its way into the reserve holdings of deposit money banks, additional new money in the form of demand deposits will tend to be created through induced bank lending. The potential increase in the money supply, therefore, is governed by the amount of new currency injected into the system, the public's preferred ratio of currency to deposits, and the effective ratio of reserves held against deposit liabilities by the lending banks.

During the 1960s, inflation was not a serious problem, but, since the early 1970s, the area has been beset by mounting inflationary pressures. (See Table 4.10.) By 1976, annual rates of inflation had reached 35 percent in Saudi Arabia and Israel; almost everywhere else, they were more than 10 percent.

---

*Deposit money banks are institutions where demand deposit liabilities serve as money. They may be publicly or privately owned.

TABLE 4.10

Money and Prices, Middle Eastern Countries, 1960s and 1970s

| | Annual Compound Rates of Change | | | | | | | |
| | Money Supply[a] | | | | Consumer Price Index | | | |
	1966-69	1969-72	1972-75	1976[b]	1966-69	1969-72	1972-75	1976[b]
Major oil states								
Algeria	25.7	15.0	22.2	21.2	—	4.3	6.4	8.3
Iran	10.7	24.2	28.8	44.7[c]	1.9	4.1	12.3	21.9[c]
Iraq	10.0	8.2	34.0	22.3[c]	3.7	4.4	7.5	11.4[c]
Kuwait	—	9.7	26.1	56.0	—	—	10.1	—
Libya	30.5	27.0	28.1	38.2	5.3	3.2	8.2	—
Saudi Arabia	10.5	17.6	55.4	100.7	2.4	3.0	24.0	35.0
Other states								
Egypt	2.9	9.9	23.5	27.8	2.7	3.0	8.2	11.5
Israel	14.0	23.5	23.9	23.4[c]	2.1	10.3	32.7	36.0[c]
Jordan	19.8	6.1	23.9	40.2	—	6.4	14.1	13.0
Lebanon	2.5	11.1	14.8[d]	—	2.5	2.2	8.5[d]	—
Morocco	11.0	12.2	20.5	22.2	0.9	3.1	9.8	8.3
Southern Yemen	-3.6	8.7	17.2	55.5[c]	—	5.2	17.3	—
Sudan	11.0	12.9	22.2	15.5	4.0	6.1	21.7	—
Syria	15.7	14.7	30.3	24.9	2.7	3.4	17.1	16.0
Tunisia	8.5	15.3	19.6	14.5	3.2	3.0	6.1	5.7
Turkey	14.8	21.5	30.6	31.8	8.3	14.0	15.8	17.2
World	8.7	11.0	12.0	14.1	4.8	5.9	12.6	11.5
Industrial countries	6.9	9.6	8.2	9.5	3.9	5.1	10.2	7.9

[a]Currency and demand deposits held by the public.
[b]Refers to the second quarter.
[c]Refers to the fourth quarter.
[d]Refers to 1972-74.

Source: International Monetary Fund, International Financial Statistics (Washington, D.C.: IMF), various issues.

External forces have also played an inflationary role. Because of the area's generally low agricultural productivity, it is sensitive to variations in the prices of imported food and agricultural products. Thus, worldwide crop failures in 1972 led to sharply increased food prices. As an illustration, in 1973, the U.S. export prices of wheat and milled rice were about twice their 1972 levels. Inflation in the industrial countries also contributed to Middle Eastern inflation through the higher cost of imported capital equipment and finished goods. Even so, these factors alone cannot account for Middle Eastern inflation, as rates in several countries were well ahead of both world and industrial country rates. The primary cause of inflation was the rapid buildup of liquidity in the area, beginning in the late 1960s.

Among the nonoil states, the governments evidently have found money creation a convenient means for financing budget deficits and, thereby, for transferring real resources to their control. While the strength of the world's demand for crude oil has protected the petroleum exporters from severe balance-of-payments problems and overly large deficits, ever-rising oil revenues have encouraged them to undertake massive development programs. (See Chapter 3.) But, in any case, accelerating government spending and monetary growth have outstripped the growth in domestic production and the capacity to import. Under these circumstances, inflationary pressures are inevitable. While price controls and other market interventions have served to loosen the connection between money and prices in the short run, serious inflationary problems cannot be avoided when money supplies grow at rates of 30, 40, or even 100 percent a year. In the area at large, the effects of excessive monetary growth have been accelerating increases in the cost of living for the public and skyrocketing expenditures by government on food imports and subsidies designed to protect the lower income classes. The enforcement of price controls encourages black market activity and worsens shortages.

The forces of inflation affect the supply and demand conditions of particular goods and services differently. While rapid monetary growth tends to stimulate demand in general, some channels of supply are better able to meet the extra requirements than others. Given foreign exchange, most lines of imported goods can expand to meet demand until port congestion and infrastructure limitations curtail further growth in supply. Thus, for a time at least, demand stimulation may not much affect the prices of goods in this category. On the other hand, supplies of goods and services that are not involved in international trade may be less elastic. Supplies of land and buildings are extreme examples of this second category. It may take years to make a significant change in the distribution of land among its alternative uses or to alter the supplies of buildings of different kinds. Increases in the total supply of useful land may be possible only in the very long run, if at all. Given such differences in supply elasticities, runaway monetary growth changes relative prices. During the early Middle Eastern boom years (1973-76), it was common for land and building rents to double annually in the major oil states and elsewhere. At the same time, the prices of imported goods increased at slower rates. The resulting change in relative prices imposed a disproportionately heavy burden on the lower income class, for whom shelter costs represent a relatively large share of household budgets. In any event, it is the poor who usually suffer most from inflation, because their money incomes are least able to increase with prices.

THE SPREAD OF FINANCE

Studies show that financial assets tend to grow in volume and variety as the scale and complexity of economic activity increases.[3] The introduction of financial instruments, usually beginning with commodity money, permits indirect exchange where only direct barter transactions had been possible. Indirect exchange eliminates the need for every potential buyer and seller to find a partner for the same good at the same time and place. Thus, freed from the confines of time and place, the market is expanded by the use of money, the basic and most important financial asset. The use of money makes saving easier and encourages the separation of the savings and investment functions. Since some members of the community are sure to be more efficient investors than others, specialization in investment by those able and willing to bear the associated risks implies a lowering of the capital/output ratio, a growing market for the savings of the rest of the community, and a rise in the investment ratio. This, in turn, leads to a proliferation of the kinds of financial assets available, as economic units specializing in investment depend more and more on the savings of the rest of the community. The concentration of capital leads to economies of scale, a further widening of the market, continued urban development, and so on.

In the process of financial development, commodity money gives way to paper currency, followed, in turn, by bank deposits as the dominant element in the money supply.* The increased acceptance and use of checks imply a developing banking system and a spreading

---

*In a study involving 36 developing countries, Khazzoom finds that the currency ratio tends to decline as the growth process continues (see J. D. Khazzoom, The Currency Ratio in Developing Countries [New York: Praeger, 1966], pp. 70-71).

of the banking habit among the people. Similarly, changes occur in the structure of securities that are outstanding. In the earlier stages of financial development, economic units specializing in investment acquire resources through the sale of securities to savers directly, but as the system matures, indirect finance becomes increasingly important. Through the sale of their own obligations to savers, financial intermediaries collect loanable funds, which they ultimately transmit to final borrowers. Other things being equal, the result is an enlargement of the volume of securities that are outstanding. Time and savings deposits in commercial banks, deposits in mutual savings banks, savings and loan shares, whole life insurance policies, pension funds, and credit union shares are familiar examples of the intermediary obligations created by this process.

In the Middle East, the major institutions in the intermediation process are deposit money banks, including both commercial and state-owned banks, which hold demand deposits. In most countries, the government has supplemented the process through the creation of specialized agricultural and industrial banks, postal savings systems, and savings banks. The development of financial intermediation in the area has resulted in a stock of financial assets that can readily be converted into cash. These quasi-money assets include time and savings deposits, postal savings deposits, and deposits in savings banks. The supply of these assets at least doubled between 1970 and 1975 in every country in the area except Algeria; in several cases, they increased four- to sixfold. (See Table 4.11.)

At the same time, the indebtedness of the public and private sectors to domestic banks of all kinds increased, in most cases by similar magnitudes. The sectoral composition of domestic bank debt varies widely in the Middle East, depending on the economic philosophy involved and the availability of petroleum revenues. Among the major oil states, domestic debt is largely private; elsewhere, the proportions vary with the extent to which economic initiative rests with the government.* Because of their higher per capita incomes and their generally limited capital absorptive capacities, the major oil states have relatively less need to incur debt. Aside from Algeria, where income from oil is more modest, the ratios of debt to the value of production are much lower in the major oil states than elsewhere.

Financial development in the Middle East has occurred unevenly. Lebanon was for many years the major financial center of the Arab

---

*In Egypt, the Sudan, and Syria, the public sector accounts for more than 60 percent of the domestic bank debt. On the other hand, in Jordan, Lebanon, Bahrain, and Tunisia, 80 percent or more is private debt.

TABLE 4.11

Indicators of Financial Development, Middle Eastern Countries, 1975

Country	Indexes of Change (1970 = 100)		Relatives— 1975	
	Quasi-Money—1975	Domestic Debt—1975	Q/M[a]	D/Y[b]
Major oil states				
Algeria	122	292	0.06	0.68
Iran	488	313	1.29	0.30
Iraq	348	93	0.41	0.06
Kuwait	205	343	1.92	0.14
Libya	618	626	0.57	0.18
Saudi Arabia	486	391	0.25	0.05
Other states				
Bahrain	572	650	1.35	0.40
Egypt	203	243	0.38	0.90
Israel	491	437	2.90	0.53
Jordan	250	293	0.27	0.51
Lebanon	254[c]	229	2.19[c]	0.60[c]
Morocco	352	233	0.11	0.55
Sudan	353	317	0.19	0.29
Syria	342	250	0.09	0.47
Tunisia	331	235	0.40	0.49
Turkey	341	379	0.25	0.38

[a]The public's primary liquid reserve assets (time, savings, and similar deposits in banks) divided by currency in the hands of the public plus demand deposits in deposit money banks.

[b]The net claims of domestic banks on the public and private sectors divided by GDP.

[c]Refers to 1974.

Source: International Monetary Fund, International Financial Statistics (Washington, D.C.: IMF), various issues.

world; in the post-World War II era, Beirut became one of the world's
leading free exchange markets. Virtually any currency was acceptable
for deposit, and there were no restrictions on the movement of funds.
Secret bank accounts were permitted. Lebanon's free economy made
Beirut an outlet for capital from all over the Arab world, as well as
a haven for short-term speculative money. Remittances from more
than 2 million expatriate Lebanese swelled the inflow of foreign exchange. Beirut brokerage firms provided linkages with European and
U.S. stock exchange and capital markets.

Lebanon's postwar financial development was stunning. The
number of banks rose from 7 in 1945 to a high of 93 in 1964; even after a tightening of banking regulations, there were 70 banks operating
there in 1974. The growth in the volume of business can be appraised
in terms of average monthly bank clearings. In 1950, monthly clearings averaged £L 30 million; by 1974, average clearings had reached
£L 1,288 million. However, the destruction wrought by the Lebanese
civil war of 1975-76 and the rise of massive payments surpluses among
the oil states have combined to bring Beirut's preeminence to an end
and to stimulate the growth of new regional centers. At mid-decade,
the potentially most important of these emerging financial centers is
located on the Gulf.

Financial developments in Bahrain and Kuwait are particularly
significant. With a combined current foreign payments surplus accruing to Saudi Arabia, Kuwait, the United Arab Emirates, and Qatar
at the rate of approximately $35 billion a year, Bahrain has emerged
as a nascent international banking center. The mainspring of Bahrain's expansion is the Offshore Banking Unit (OBU). Attracted by
the absence of personal and corporate income taxes, exchange controls, and reserve requirements on offshore business, by mid-1977,
32 major international banks had established branches to do business
freely with all but Bahraini nationals. This licensing qualification was
intended to protect the small domestic market from overbanking,
while, at the same time, permitting the growth of a high-income service industry engaged in channeling excess oil funds to overseas borrowers. By mid-1977, $9 billion of loanable funds had found their
way into OBU time deposits.

Whereas Bahrain's goal is development as a regional money
market a long-term capital market is emerging in Kuwait. Since 1973,
dozens of Kuwaiti investment houses have been established, and Arab
Gulf currency bonds are being floated to provide outlets for the funds
of wealthy individuals and firms who wish to make long-term investments rather than hold less profitable bank deposits. Given the size
of the annual surpluses that can be forecast, there is good reason to
expect the Gulf region to develop into a financial center of major importance in the years ahead.

SOME CONCLUDING OBSERVATIONS

In the realm of finance, the impact of oil is starkly apparent. The states with large per capita reserve holdings are presently free from the problems of deficit finance. Their mineral royalty and enterprise incomes provide them with a relative abundance of foreign exchange; recently, they have become major sources of international assistance. Meanwhile, the nonoil states are deeply involved in the problems of deficit spending and are becoming increasingly dependent on the major oil states for assistance. In short, it is the abundance or absence of oil that divides the area into two groups—the one financially affluent and politically influential and the other relatively poor and increasingly dependent. In terms of factors of production other than capital, however, both groups are poor. Both share the common goals of economic diversification and real development.

The recent rise in oil revenue is providing the whole region with a unique but transitory opportunity to pursue these goals. But as state spending has risen, the region has been beset by a rising tide of inflationary pressure. The acute shortages of infrastructure and human skills have prevented real output growth from matching financial outlays. In addition, growth in the public sector's control of resources has strained the capacities of semimodern bureaucracies, so that planning and implementation have suffered. Not only has the absolute level of prices been pushed up rapidly but relative prices have been distorted as well.

Among the nonoil states, the problem of allocative efficiency is probably compounded by their heavy reliance on indirect taxation for revenue. Sales taxes and customs duties typically range from 3 percent up to 60 percent, although customs duties on luxury goods may reach 200 percent ad valorem. Selective exemptions from duties are given to members of special groups, including the households of ruling families, religious hierarchies, and the importers of officially favored goods. The result is a tendency toward inequity and regressivity in tax burdens. Furthermore, the uneven alteration of after-tax prices means that production and consumption are shifted toward those inputs and products that have been relatively cheapened; after-tax-price ratios will probably not reflect true relative scarcities. Thus, heavy reliance on indirect taxes most likely contributes to inefficiency in resource allocation.

In conclusion, a genuine settlement of the Arab-Israeli controversy would free resources for civilian use and reduce the heavy cost of military competition now being borne by the confrontation states. By assuming that excessive military expenditures had instead been directed into capital formation, some indication of the opportunity cost of recent military effort is obtained. (See Table 4.12.) These cal-

TABLE 4.12

Opportunity Cost of Military Spending, Major Confrontation States
in the Arab-Israeli Controversy, 1973-75
(millions of 1974 U.S. dollars)

Major Confrontation States	Excessive Military Expenditures[a] ÷	Incremental Capital/ Output Ratio =	Forgone Civilian Value Product
Egypt	2,485[b]	3.1	802
Israel	8,844[b]	2.4	3,685
Syria	1,031[b]	2.2	469

[a]Excessive military spending is defined as the difference between a country's actual military expenditure and the level that represents the fraction of GNP spent for military purposes by the developing world as a whole.

[b]Figures are cumulative totals for the three years 1973 through 1975.

Sources: U.S. Arms Control and Disarmament Agency, World Military Expenditures and Arms Transfers 1966-75 (Washington, D.C.: USACDA, 1976); and International Bank for Reconstruction and Development, World Tables, 1975 (Washington, D.C.: IBRD, 1976).

culations suggest that, had military spending in 1973-75 been limited to the average of the developing countries as a whole and the residual resources been used for real capital formation, potential production in Israel would be nearly $4 billion greater. Under these assumptions, Egypt and Syria would also be substantially better off. The estimates assume that other basic economic relationships implied by historic capital/output ratios continue to prevail. Over the years, these forgone value products represent serious losses to economies struggling to improve their welfare. The future incomes of these countries will forever be lower than they might have been had fewer resources been used for military purposes and more for capital accumulation.

NOTES

1.   Hisham B. Sharabi, <u>Nationalism and Revolution in the Arab World</u> (Princeton, N.J.: D. Van Nostrand, 1966), pp. 15-18; and P. J. Vatikiotis, <u>Conflict in the Middle East</u> (London: Allen and Unwin, 1971), pp. 3-13.

2.   For an elaboration of this process, see Mancur Olson, "Rapid Growth as a Destabilizing Force," <u>Journal of Economic History</u> 23, no. 4 (1963): 529-52.

3.   Especially significant in this regard is the work of Goldsmith. See Raymond W. Goldsmith, <u>Financial Structure and Development</u> (New Haven, Conn.: Yale University Press, 1969).

5

THE MIDDLE EASTERN
OIL TRADE

The postwar oil boom has made fortunes for individuals, firms, and governments in many parts of the world, but especially in the Middle East. Continuous discovery of new resources gave the region a rising share of the world's proved reserves in an era of ever-increasing dependence on oil as an energy source.* These shifts in the sources of supply and in energy demand have made rights to the area's low-cost reserves the keys to wealth and market power.†

THE MAJOR FIRMS IN THE MIDDLE EAST

Since the rise of John D. Rockefeller's Standard Oil Company in 1870, the world oil industry has been dominated by a few large integrated firms. As vertical integration promised cost reductions through economies of scale, and as the elimination of rivals provided control over prices, Rockefeller's domination of the U.S. refining capacity and pipelines permitted his successful conquest of the new industry without control of crude oil at its source. In the United States, the wide distribution of property rights assured control of the

---

*Proved reserves are those recoverable under existing economic and operating conditions.

†In 1949, the Middle East contained 45 percent of total world reserves; by 1976, its share was 61 percent. During this period, the world's energy consumption increased more than threefold, from 2,036 million to 6,432 million tons of oil equivalent, and oil's share in total energy supply rose from 18 to 45 percent.

oil fields by a large number of firms. In the Middle East, after D'Arcy's arrangements with the government of Iran, the concession system offered access to the region's great oil reservoirs to a few, and this reinforced the tendency toward an oligopolistic structure in the world oil industry. (See section on Petroleum Resources in Chapter 1 for discussion of D'Arcy's arrangements with Iran.) For many years, the world oil trade was dominated by seven vertically integrated international firms—the famous seven sisters.* The distribution of their concessionary interests in the Middle East is shown in Table 5.1.

With regard to the corporate arrangements most often used in developing Middle Eastern oil, the actual search, development, and production operations were conducted by affiliates, which, in turn, were jointly owned by several major firms. By participating in the ownership of these operating companies, with various combinations of other firms, each of the seven was assured access to virtually all of the reservoirs of the area, at prices mutually agreed upon by them. While somewhat different arrangements emerged in North Africa, this pattern prevailed around the Gulf.

The development of the Iraqi oil industry began in 1925 when a concession was granted to the Turkish Petroleum Company, soon to be called the Iraq Petroleum Company (IPC). The parent companies were BP, Royal-Dutch/Shell, Compagnie Française des Pétroles, Standard Oil of New Jersey, Mobil, and the Gulbenkian estate.† Through securing three major concessions, this group came to control the petroleum rights to virtually the whole of Iraq. Affiliates of IPC held concession rights in Qatar (1953) and Abu Dhabi (1939). The group also owned an affiliate that held a concession in Oman (1937). Lack of promise there encouraged most of the IPC members to withdraw, leaving the interest to Shell (85 percent), the Gulbenkian estate (5 percent), and the Compagnie Française des Pétroles (10 percent).

In the history of concessionary interests in the Middle East, it is probable that none represents a more contentious and strife-ridden relationship than the one between IPC and the Iraqi government. The relationship ended finally on June 1, 1972, with the nationalization of IPC assets by the government of Iraq.

---

*Because of its extensive participation in joint operating companies in the Middle East, the Compagnie Française des Pétroles could be included as an eighth major firm.

†Calouste S. Gulbenkian was an Armenian promoter who interested the Ottoman and British governments in Mesopotamian oil prior to World War I.

TABLE 5.1

Major International Firms in the Middle East, 1970

Host Country	British Petroleum	Compagnie Française des Pétroles	Gulf Oil	Royal-Dutch/Shell	Socony Mobil Oil	Standard Oil of New Jersey	Standard Oil (Exxon) Company of California	Texas Company (Texaco)
Abu Dhabi	X	X		X	X	X		
Algeria		X		X	X			
Bahrain							X	X
Dubai (offshore)	X	X						
Iran	X	X	X	X	X	X	X	X
Iraq	X	X		X	X	X		
Kuwait	X		X					
Libya	X			X	X	X	X	X
Oman		X		X	X			
Qatar	X	X		X	X	X		
Saudi Arabia					X	X	X	X
Turkey					X	X		X

Source: The Middle East and North Africa, 1970–71 (London: Europa Publications, 1970).

101

An earlier attempt at nationalization on the Arabian Gulf had been unsuccessful when, in 1951, the Iranian government nationalized the Anglo-Iranian Company, heir to the D'Arcy concession. The Iranian government found, however, that it was not equipped to compete with the major firms, who controlled the market outlets for petroleum products. As sales declined, the loss of revenue forced the government to accept the formation of a consortium to lift, refine, and distribute oil. Participation shares in the consortium were BP (formerly Anglo-Iranian), 40 percent; Standard Oil Company of New Jersey, Mobil, Standard Oil Company of California, Gulf, and Texaco, 7 percent each; Royal-Dutch/Shell, 14 percent; the Compagnie Française des Pétroles, 6 percent; and the Iricon Agency, 5 percent.* Although legal title to the original concession was retained by a government firm, the National Iranian Oil Company, the consortium had control of the utilization of the resources throughout the 1950s and 1960s. Two operating companies, one for exploration and production and another for refining, managed the assets of the parent companies on a cost plus fee basis. Products were marketed through trading companies owned by the consortium. In 1973, the Iranian government took 100 percent control of the industry for the National Iranian Oil Company.

In 1933, Standard Oil of California was granted a concession by Saudi Arabia in its Eastern Province. Texaco acquired an interest in 1936, and in 1947, Standard Oil of New Jersey and Mobil acquired shares. Until 1972, these companies owned the Arabian American Oil Company (Aramco), the operating company, as follows: Standard Oil of California, Texaco, and Standard Oil of New Jersey, 30 percent each, and Mobil, 10 percent. At its largest, the Aramco concession covered 440,000 square miles, but postwar relinquishments reduced it to 125,000. The latter area contains the richest oil deposits known at the present time. Saudi Arabia negotiated a 25 percent participation share in Aramco in 1972 and increased its share to 60 percent in 1974. By 1975, negotiations on complete nationalization were under way. These moves paralleled similar trends toward full government ownership in Kuwait and the Gulf emirates.

Kuwait granted its major concession in 1934 to Kuwait Oil Company (KOC), a company owned by Gulf and BP at 50 percent each. The original concession of 6,000 square miles was reduced to 2,200 in 1962 to make room for a state firm, the Kuwait National Petroleum Company. Full nationalization of KOC was completed in 1975.

The French government undertook oil exploration in Algeria in 1952 through permits issued to form operating companies. Shares in

---

*The Iricon Agency included nine smaller U.S. companies.

these companies were held by the French Bureau de Recherches de Pétroles and Regie Autonome des Pétroles, the Compagnie Française des Pétroles, and Royal-Dutch/Shell. Oil was struck in 1956. As part of its drive for petroleum self-sufficiency, France poured large amounts of capital into Algerian oil development. Under the terms of the 1962 agreements between the French government and the FLN, Algeria acquired French oil interests but agreed to work out a system of cooperation with the French in exploitation of Algerian mineral resources. Under the Accord Pétrolier of July 1965, the parties attempted to cooperate in oil production through two companies: Societe Nationale de Transport et de Commercialisation des Hydrocarbures (SONATRACH), an Algerian national firm, and the Societe Pétroliere Française en Algeria, representing French interests. In addition, several European and U.S. firms were permitted to engage in various stages of production in Algeria. These arrangements proved to be transitory. Step by step, the Algerian government has moved to reduce foreign petroleum activity. In 1967, Algeria nationalized the Standard Oil and Mobil marketing networks and, a year later, several other distribution organizations. This and the purchase of BP's distribution network in 1966 gave SONATRACH full control of the internal market. Disagreements with the French over taxing, pricing, and investment issues led to the end of cooperation. In February 1971, Algeria nationalized 51 percent of French interests, which had produced the preponderance of Algerian oil. In addition, the government nationalized all foreign-owned natural gas companies and pipelines but accepted the obligation to pay compensation. Algeria now has effective control of its oil resources.

The development of the Algerian petroleum sector stands in sharp contrast to the experience of the Gulf states. In the latter, the development initiative was in the hands of a few large international firms, which undertook to exploit concession rights to enormous tracts of land. In Algeria, exploitation rights have been held mostly by states: first, the French state; then, the Algerian and French states in combination; and, finally, the Algerian state.

The case of Libya provides yet another approach to the exploitation of mineral resources. The high quality of its oil, its proximity to Europe, and the more competitive pattern of development it chose served to lift it to major exporter status in a very few years during the 1960s. In 1955, before any major operations had begun, the Libyan government passed a law outlining the terms under which it would issue exploration licenses for one year. At the end of the period, the licensee would be eligible to bid for a concession that might be held for a maximum of 50 years over a territory that would gradually be reduced in size to about a quarter of the original. Incentives to compete were provided to foreign firms through depreciation allowances and tax inducements. Major oil strikes occurred in 1959, and by 1960, 19 companies held exploration licenses. By 1968, the number had risen to 37. Among the large international firms, Standard Oil of New Jersey emerged as a leading producer. Reflecting the more competitive framework chosen by Libya for developing oil resources, the other leading producer was the Oasis group, comprised of Amerada, Marathon, and Continental, three U.S. independents, and Royal-Dutch/Shell. Occidental Petroleum was another important producer. In 1971, Libya nationalized a fraction of BP's holdings in retaliation for Britain's countenancing of Iran's seizure of three Arabian Gulf islands.* In 1973, Libya took control of 51 percent of the entire industry.

Although alternative arrangements for development existed, it should be recognized that, by the 1960s, all of the major exporting states were moving toward greater participation in decision making by host governments. This took the form of state enterprise in exploration and production, as well as nationalization or direct participation in the producing affiliates of the international firms.[1]

MARKET STRUCTURE

As a tool of analysis, the oligopoly model of pricing and output seems best suited for considering the behavior of the major international oil firms. With major firms being few in number, the demand faced by the individual firm is assumed to be influenced by the price and output decisions of its rivals. If the behavior of the rival is accurately predicted, the demand curve faced by the individual firm can be estimated, and a profit-maximizing price and output can be determined. On the other hand, if the behavior of the rivals is not predictable, the maximization of profits is unlikely. Therefore, the oligopolistic international major firms are assumed to have a mutual interest in price stability and in predictable market shares.

While the international major firms should not be characterized as being a formal cartel, their past behavior suggests the case of oligopoly, in which tacit, informal agreements are relied upon to reduce mutual uncertainty. The core of the world petroleum market was for many years the United States, and, to a significant extent, the world structure represents the international extension of the imperfectly competitive conditions of the U.S. industry.

In 1919, the Texas Railroad Commission undertook the regulation of output in order to stabilize prices. As the procedure developed

---

*These were Abu Musa, Greater Tumbs, and Lesser Tumbs.

over the next two decades, the commission joined with representatives of the producers, truckers, and refiners to estimate the monthly demand for Texas crude oil. Also, they estimated the maximum efficient rate of flow (mer) for each oil pool in Texas, so that the amount of oil that would be produced at a given rate of capacity utilization could be determined. Given this information, the anticipated monthly demand was prorated among the wells in order to balance supply and demand. The management of each well was assigned some percentage of its capacity that it might produce in the coming month. Although the participants disavowed price setting, given market demand, the control of output implied the setting of an equilibrium price. Historically, these procedures served to maintain aggregate excess capacity, thereby holding U.S. crude oil prices above their competitive level.[2] Even so, there is a case for special institutional arrangements in oil production. The development of the east Texas fields makes this clear.

The pattern of development of U.S. oil fields has been formed by the rule of capture. As this common law principle gives the title of oil to the one who lifts it, it follows that rights to oil are a function of surface drilling rights. Since units of surface property do not conform to subsurface mineral distribution, the rule of capture leads to the drilling of many more wells than are necessary for the best technical exploitation of a given pool of oil. In the case of east Texas, a strike in 1930, yielding 20,000 barrels a day, led to a rush for oil leases. In a year, 3,600 wells were drilled and more than 1 million barrels produced. After 25 years, more than 3 billion barrels of oil had been produced in an area 5 or 6 miles wide and 40 miles long by some 559 operators owning 2,567 leases.[3] Excessive drilling reduced the potential of what was probably the greatest field of the United States by wasting reservoir pressure and encouraging water encroachment.

One important reason why Middle Eastern oil is relatively cheap is that the concession system tended to give single or a few firms drilling rights to individual reservoirs and to avoid the overdrilling encouraged by widely distributed surface property rights. When management is unified, the technical characteristics of each particular oil pool can be considered in choosing the most efficient number and spacing of wells. Today, most Middle Eastern wells are still on natural drive, while in the United States, nearly all of the wells are dependent on more expensive pumping techniques of various kinds.

These differences are reflected in contemporary unit costs. Based on expenditure estimates by the Chase Manhattan Bank, capital expenses incurred to maintain or expand production in the United States averaged $1.54 a barrel in the 1960s but averaged only $0.10 in the Arabian Gulf. As crude oil production is capital intensive, labor costs are a relatively minor expense consideration. Vast size, low unit cost of production, and proximity to ocean-shipping facilities give the Middle Eastern oil fields their present commercial advantage. Underlying this market power are institutional as well as natural factors.*

An early attempt to establish an international cartel occurred in 1928 when the heads of the Anglo-Persian Oil Company (later, Anglo-Iranian and BP), Standard Oil of New Jersey, and Royal-Dutch/Shell reached what has been called the "As-Is Agreement." Noting that major producers seeking to increase sales at the expense of their rivals led to increased production and falling prices, they agreed to accept the existing market shares and to secure a more profitable utilization of existing capacity. The firms agreed to sell oil at a common price and to obtain supplies from the cheapest source. Affiliates in short supply should satisfy their requirements from other major companies having surplus capacity in the area rather than shipping oil from some other region of the world in which a given company might have excess capacity of its own. In this way, price competition would be eliminated, output would be stabilized, and transportation costs would be reduced.

At the time of the As-Is Agreement, the United States represented by far the largest oil-producing and -consuming area of the world, so that the cartel chose to base world oil prices on the Texas Gulf price. Under the As-Is Agreement, producers charged free on board (f.o.b.) port-of-shipment prices equal to the Texas Gulf price. For oil delivered to port of entry, purchasers were charged cost, insurance, and freight (c.i.f.) prices equal to the Texas price plus a standard markup, drawn from a schedule of agreed-upon freight rates

---

*In retrospect, the intervention of the Texas Railroad Commission represents a less than ideal solution to a classic case of what is referred to in economics as the common pool problem. When a great many owners share imprecise rights to a single pool (of oil, fish, wild game, and so forth), each has an incentive to extract as much as possible before it is taken by competitors. The end result is that the pool is drained as rapidly as the circumstances permit, and the total recoverable amount of the resource is reduced by wasteful practices. Common pool situations are among the rare cases in economics in which competition is theoretically undesirable. The actual outcome in the United States has been neither as efficient as the alternative provided by unified management nor as destructive as would have been the case under competition. Had unregulated competition prevailed, prices would initially have been lower, but the pools would have been drained sooner.

from each port of shipment to each port of entry. In this way, differences in prices caused by fluctuations in tanker rates and differences in method of shipment were eliminated. The prices charged were not open market prices but, rather, intracompany billings, which were, essentially, bookkeeping transactions. Under these arrangements, windfall profits were implied when the actual costs of oil were less than the Texas Gulf price and when the scheduled freight allowance exceeded the actual cost of freight. By the end of the 1930s, the big three had been joined by Gulf Oil, the Texas Company, and Standard Oil of California as major international producers. Great new fields had been developed in Venezuela, the Middle East, and Indonesia. By 1944, the British Admiralty was disturbed at having to pay the Texas Gulf price plus phantom freight for the purchases in the Arabian Gulf. Under pressure from the British government, the companies reduced the price of Arabian Gulf oil to the price level of the Texas Gulf. In effect, the Arabian Gulf was established as a price basing point.

BARGAINING FOR RENT

The world crude oil industry may be conceived of as a collection of individual oil pools. For the individual pool, the incremental or marginal cost of another barrel of oil rises in the long run as more oil and gas are taken. Initially, a pool may yield oil on natural drive, as oil is forced to the surface by gas pressure, but, eventually, a second stage of production is reached in which production requires some form of pumping or artificial lift. Therefore, as cumulative production rises, a firm exploiting a particular oil pool will be forced to make expenditures on additional equipment. Also, a firm will be required to incur costs in searching for new pools of oil in order to offset the relentless rise of operating and development costs as existing pools are depleted. A continuously expanding search for oil implies deeper drilling and exploration offshore and in more remote areas. Search costs can be expected to rise. Thus, in the long run, the individual firm produces under increasing marginal cost conditions. The price must cover operating costs and, in addition, provide a rate of return on invested capital sufficient to induce the firm to undertake development of known pools of oil and the search for new ones.

Under competitive conditions, the industry supply price schedule would measure the unit costs that must necessarily be incurred at various rates of production. The marginal cost of the industry is that of the highest cost pool at any given rate of output.[4]

In the short run, producers in the industry have insufficient time to expand capacity of available pools or to search for new pools

in response to price changes. Under these circumstances, the firms'
minimum supply price is the necessary incremental cost of supplying
another barrel with existing facilities.

Economic profits accrued to firms in the Middle East because
of productivity and site advantages and because of the imperfectly
competitive marketing conditions that actually prevailed. When
large economic profits were earned by firms, host governments were
encouraged to seek profit-sharing arrangements. When a few large
firms produced oil from a few large pools owned by a few states at
prices far above necessary production costs, as in the Middle East,
the oligopolistic conditions lend themselves to analysis in terms of
the standard bilateral monopoly model. Variations of this model are
used in Figures 5.1 and 5.2 to consider the conflict potential that is
an inherent feature of Middle Eastern oil production and exchange.

Figure 5.1 applies to a hypothetical case in which a multina-
tional oil firm holds concession rights to a nation's only oil reservoir.
Search and development costs have been met by the firm, and oil has
been struck. The firm's short-run marginal cost curve, MC_0, measures the necessary addition to total operating cost incurred in the
production of another daily barrel at various possible rates of output.
Necessary incremental costs are assumed to be constant up to the
point at which capacity is fully utilized, after which they become in-
finite. No amount of spending on variable factors will increase output once the productive limits of the existing facilities have been
reached.

The demand for crude oil is derived from the demand for petroleum products. This being the case, the firm's marginal revenue
product curve (MRP) constitutes its demand for crude oil as a factor
of production.* The firm will wish to "purchase" crude oil from nature as long as MRP exceeds MC_0. In the case depicted in Figure
5.1, the firm will wish to lift crude oil at the rate of OB_0 barrels a
day, where MC_0 = MRP at point C. The firm's cost of crude oil ac-
quisition is $OACB_0$, whereas its revenues are $ODCB_0$. Its economic
profit is ACD.

In the situation described in Figure 5.1, lifting crude oil is
highly profitable; revenues are large in relation to costs. Eventually,
the host government will become aware of the large economic profit
being earned. It will wish to charge rent in order to share in the surplus. The capture of all of the surplus represents the maximum possible objective of the government. Theoretically, it could do this

---

*MRP equals the marginal revenue of generalized petroleum
products production multiplied by the marginal productivity of crude
oil in the production of petroleum products.

FIGURE 5.1

Concession Model

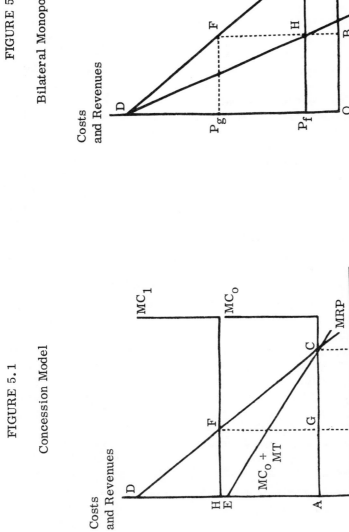

Source: Constructed by the author.

FIGURE 5.2

Bilateral Monopoly Model

Source: Constructed by the author.

109

either by perfect price discrimination, shading unit charges along the demand curve to absorb all of the spread between MRP and MC_O, or by a 100 percent tax on economic profits. The firm might resist such proposals by threatening to switch production elsewhere or by threatening to disinvest in the long run. In response, the host government might threaten to reduce concession rights and to invite other firms into its territory or use the ultimate threat of nationalization. Actually, neither side gains economically from a cessation of production. The firm may not have low-cost alternative reservoirs available, and the country may find downstream operations, refining, and marketing, difficult if not impossible after nationalization. Some compromise is therefore likely. A 50-50 profit-sharing arrangement is common in such cases. Suppose the firm and the host government agree to a tax on economic profit at the rate of 50 percent. Profits would be divided equally between the two sides. In Figure 5.1, the firm's marginal cost plus marginal tax liability schedule, $MC_O + MT$, is found by dividing the vertical distance between the MRP and MC_O curves in half. The $MC_O + MT$ curve divides the total area of economic profits into two equal parts. The firm's after-tax profit is ECD, and the country's rental income is ACE. As the firm takes its tax liability into account, the marginal conditions will not be disturbed in the short run, and the optimal output will remain OB_O barrels per day. To the left of OB_O, $MC_O + MT$ is less than MRP, and the firm has an incentive to increase production. To the right of OB_O, $MC_O + MT$ exceeds MRP, so that the firm has an incentive to reduce output. At OB_O, $MC + MT = MRP$, and thus, it remains the optimal rate of production after the tax has been levied.

An alternative method of rent collection might be a charge levied on each barrel of oil produced. In effect, this would be excise taxation. This approach influences the marginal fiscal conditions, because marginal cost is increased by the amount of tax. For example, in Figure 5.1, should the government succeed in collecting a per barrel charge of FG, the marginal tax paid cost schedule would rise to MC_1. The firm would have an incentive to cut back production to OB_1, where $MC_1 = MRP$. The firm's necessary costs are reduced from $OACB_O$ to $OAGB_1$, but its tax-paid costs rise to $OHFB_1$ and its profits become HFD. The host country's rent is now AGFH.

In consideration of these alternatives, consumers of petroleum products are likely to be better off with an income tax. Since the excise tax approach constricts production, other things being the same, prices of finished products will tend to be higher than they would be under income taxation.

If a host country were to nationalize the assets of a major oil firm, undertaking the production of crude oil and its sale to the former producer, the situation would approximate the case depicted in

Figure 5.2. The marginal cost schedule is now the government oil production agency's short-run minimum supply price schedule, MC_g. This curve also would be the firm's marginal resource cost curve, MRC_f, a schedule showing the minimum prices that must be paid to bring forth additional amounts of crude oil. The monopsony firm would wish to maximize profits by purchasing OB_f daily barrels, the flow at which $MRC_f = MRP_f$ at point C. It would offer to pay no more than OP_f for each of the OB_f barrels, since that is the price that just covers the necessary cost of the marginal barrel to the government. On the other hand, the government production agency is now a monopolistic seller of oil. From its point of view, the firm's demand schedule, MRP_f, is the agency's average revenue schedule, AR_g. Given AR_g, the government oil production agency could calculate its marginal revenue schedule, MR_g. As a profit-maximizing producer, it would wish to produce OB_g daily barrels, where its marginal revenue is equal to its marginal cost at point H, and it would wish to charge OP_g per barrel, the full value of the marginal barrel to the buyer at point F and the most that the firm could be expected to pay. The actual price and output are theoretically indeterminate and must be settled by negotiation. The actual price will be between OP_f and OP_g. The actual output will be within OB_g and OB_f. The maximum profits possible for the firm are P_fCD, whereas the production agency's maximum potential profits are P_fHFP_g. This exercise provides a background for evaluating actual price determination.

DEVELOPMENT OF MIDDLE
EASTERN CRUDE OIL PRICES

With the removal of price controls at the end of World War II, U.S. crude oil prices more than doubled within three years. At the same time, Arabian Gulf prices were increased, but a differential was maintained. For example, in 1949, the price of Saudi Arabian light crude was $1.75 a barrel, as compared with $2.50 for oil of like quality on the U.S. Gulf coast. Thereafter, until 1960, Arabian Gulf prices were geared to U.S. Gulf prices. The two price structures moved together, but, at the same time, the gap between the U.S. and Arabian Gulf posted prices was widened. These price relationships reflected the tremendous rise in Middle Eastern capacity, the lower cost of production there, and the very rapid rise in output. The area's proved reserves, including those of North Africa, rose from 32.7 billion barrels in 1949 to 408.8 billion barrels in 1970, while in the same period, the combined reserves of the United States and Venezuela rose from 32.2 billion to only 51.0 billion barrels. By 1970, the Middle East accounted for well over 60 percent of world reserves. [5]

The great rise in Middle Eastern capacity and the lower costs there made it increasingly attractive for the major firms to switch production to that area. From 1952 to 1970, Middle Eastern output rose at an average annual rate of nearly 13 percent, while the output of the United States rose at a rate of less than 3 percent. During the period, oil from the Middle East rapidly enlarged its position in total world supply (Figure 5.3).

To utilize this growing capacity and output, the major firms could be expected to lower their internal transfer prices, as well as the prices charged outsiders. As the profitable relationship between the price and cost of Middle Eastern crude oil became known, the host governments grew increasingly dissatisfied with the existing payment system. Initial lump sum payments plus relatively modest royalty payments per ton of output were the general practices among the older concessions.

In 1950, Aramco and the Saudi Arabian government negotiated a 50-50 profit-sharing agreement. Under the new arrangement, Aramco agreed to pay the government half of its net accounting profits. The firm's royalty payment of five shillings a ton could be used as a credit toward its tax obligation to the government. While this agreement was being negotiated, Aramco received permission from the U.S. Treasury to treat payments to the Saudi government as a credit against its liability under the U.S. corporation tax laws. In effect, Aramco was permitted to calculate its tax obligation to the Saudi government before paying corporate income taxes to the U.S. government and to receive a tax credit for these payments against its U.S. tax obligations. The host government gained at the expense of the U.S. Treasury, while the net effect on the firm was nil. The 50-50 profit-sharing arrangement quickly spread to other countries and became the standard payment system in the area. The increased revenue available to the host governments should have reduced friction between the countries and the oil firms operating in the Middle East. Any gains of this nature were quickly eroded, however, by the problems inherent in the new system.

Under the former arrangements, the royalty obligation per ton of output was the basis of government income, and official interest tended to be focused on output, as the government's revenue varied with the volume of production. Under the 50-50 plan, government income was influenced by company costs and prices, as well as the volume of production. Friction between firms and host governments increased, as the latter now had an economic stake in entrepreneurial decisions. Host governments questioned the firms' cost-accounting conventions, as these influenced the allocation of the overhead and other costs of integrated enterprise between the Middle East and other regions.[6] The question of the price was even more fundamental.

FIGURE 5.3

Development of World Crude Oil Supplies, 1952–76

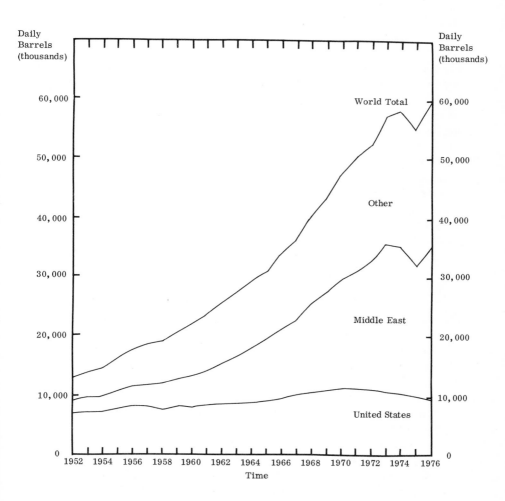

Sources: American Petroleum Institute, Petroleum Facts and Figures (Washington, D.C.: API, 1971); and BP Statistical Review of the World Oil Industry, 1976 (London: British Petroleum Company, 1977).

In the early 1950s, most of the oil lifted in the Middle East was moved to higher stages of production through the integrated major firms. Relatively small amounts of oil entered the open market in sales to outsiders. Posted prices were tax reference prices, but they also represented the prices producers were prepared to charge for tanker cargo lots. Before the 1956 Suez War, posted prices approximated equilibrium prices, but later in the decade, excess supply conditions emerged. As new independent producers entered the field and capacity outran the growth in demand, oil sold in the open market at a discount below posted prices. In 1959, the United States imposed import quotas, ostensibly to encourage domestic exploration and development. Whatever the intent, this policy served to screen off the U.S. market from cheaper Middle Eastern crude oil and to buttress excess supply conditions in the eastern hemisphere.

The posted price for crude oil was lowered from $2.08 per barrel in 1958 to $1.80 in 1960, and the governments responded by forming the Organization of Petroleum Exporting Countries (OPEC). At this stage, OPEC represented an attempt to organize countervailing power against the oligopolistic major firms. Its original members were Iran, Iraq, Kuwait, Saudi Arabia, and Venezuela. Subsequently, Qatar, Libya, Indonesia, the United Arab Emirates, Algeria, Nigeria, Ecuador, and Gabon (an associate member) were admitted. The initial objective of the organization was to restore posted prices to the 1958 level. Although they failed to achieve this objective immediately, they succeeded in checking any further decline in posted prices and in making them an issue for negotiation. In reality, the 50-50 profit-sharing plan was essentially a system of excise taxation, with posted prices, minus unit cost, multiplied by 50 percent, producing a tax per unit of output. With the continued downward drift in market prices during the 1960s, posted prices became simply tax reference prices.

A reform achieved in 1964 by OPEC, which had the effect of raising the relative shares of the host governments, was the "expensing" of royalties. This reform permitted the deduction of the contractual royalties due the governments as a cost in the determination of revenue shares under the 50-50 formula. The host governments received 50 percent of formula profits plus the royalty.* Prior to this reform, royalties were not treated as an expense and could be counted toward satisfying the firms' tax liability.

Another factor that increased the economic power of the exporting countries was their success in requiring the major firms to relinquish concession territories so that their rights provided access to

---

*For an example, assume a posted price of $1.80 per barrel, with an operating cost of $0.10 and a royalty of $0.25 per barrel:

small fractions of their former territories. This reallocation of rights gave the states the opportunity to enter new and improved agreements with foreign firms or to exploit the territories with their own national firms. By the end of the 1960s, Iran, Iraq, Kuwait, Saudi Arabia, Libya, and Algeria had set up state firms to engage in exploration, production, and refining of petroleum and natural gas. The latter category included petrochemicals and fertilizers. As a result of this increased accessibility, European and Japanese firms entered into various kinds of joint enterprise arrangements with Middle Eastern state firms. Independent operators became increasingly important in the area. As these firms increased output, the major firms were forced to expand production in order to protect their market shares. Thus, the entry of the independent firms contributed to the growth of excess supply conditions and weakened the ability of the major firms to maintain prices. Nonetheless, this is not to say that lifting crude oil did not continue to be a profitable business for the major firms.

NATURE OF THE GAINS

The major oil firms have been hesitant in revealing their profits from crude oil production, but such evidence as is available indicates that rates of return of invested capital were high. In 1961, OPEC commissioned a study of company profits by A. D. Little. Although the findings have never been officially released, they have been revealed in several published debates and studies and show that average returns on net assets in the Gulf area ranged from 61 to 114 percent for the period 1956-60.[7]

It would be a mistake to take these data as literal indications of yields among the main areas of the eastern hemisphere, for the major

Posted price	$1.800
Less:	
Operating cost	0.10
Royalty	0.25
Equals notational profit	1.450
Times 50 percent tax	0.500
Equals firm's tax obligation	0.725
Plus:	
Operating cost	0.10
Royalty	0.25
Equals tax paid cost to firm	1.075
Government revenue: tax plus royalty	0.975

firms are integrated enterprises, whose activities range from lifting crude oil to marketing refined products. The net earnings they choose to report at each stage of production are largely a matter of accounting convention. A higher transfer price for crude set by one affiliate in the Middle East implies a higher cost and a smaller profit margin for another affiliate or the parent company producing finished goods in Europe. Measuring profitability in terms of return on net worth, data supplied by the First National City Bank show that global returns earned by the seven major firms in the eastern hemisphere were quite modest during the decade just prior to the restructuring of the industry in 1973. (See Table 5.2.) This is so even in relation to yields in domestic U.S. manufacturing in general. Obviously, the biases of the analyst, the measure of return chosen for use, as well as accounting practices in general, influence the results of any inquiry into yields on oil company investment. In an industry where financial information has been closely guarded, estimated rates of return are inevitably controversial. On balance, however, the conclusion is that returns on invested capital in lifting crude oil were relatively high in the Middle East, although overall yields on integrated operations were unexceptional in the eastern hemisphere at large.

Under the concessionary system, oil reserves provided an income stream to the host governments primarily in the form of tax and royalty payments from the producing firms. The data show that through time, rates of growth of output and revenue have varied widely. (See Table 5.3.) During the early years of development, high potential newcomers, such as Libya and Abu Dhabi, attained high rates of output growth, but as their oil sectors approached maturity, these rates declined. Throughout the postwar years, government oil revenue has tended to outrun production. In the early 1950s, revenues moved ahead of output, as the 50-50 profit-sharing arrangements greatly increased the governments' per barrel income. In the later period, the more effective use of their inherent negotiating strength enabled the governments to secure higher posted prices and other changes, which greatly increased their revenues, while the world recession and voluntary conservation slowed output. Although per barrel payments to host governments rose during the 1960s, these increases were relatively modest. With posted prices held at $1.80 per barrel, gains for host governments depended on procedural changes, such as the expensing of royalties. During the 1950s and 1960s, research and development (R&D) operations of the private firms kept reserves expanding at the same time output was growing rapidly; in the 1970s, proved reserves have, in certain instances, begun to shrink.*

---

*This shrinkage of reserves is confined to Libya and Kuwait. Since these are small, high-income countries, with very limited capi-

TABLE 5.2

Changing Shares in Net Revenue per Barrel, Eastern Hemisphere, 1962-72

Item	1962	1964	1966	1968	1970	1972
Payments to host governments (U.S. dollars)	0.709	0.752	0.771	0.834	0.865	1.341
Per barrel earnings of major firms (U.S. dollars)	0.531	0.432	0.411	0.406	0.336	0.283
Firms' earnings per barrel relative to payments to host governments (percent)	75.0	57.0	53.0	49.0	39.0	21.0
Firms' rate of return on net worth (percent)	13.1	11.1	11.5	12.5	11.8	10.0

Note: The data cover the eastern hemisphere operations of BP, Standard Oil of New Jersey (Exxon), Gulf Oil, Socony Mobil, Royal-Dutch/Shell, Standard Oil of California, and the Texas Company (Texaco).

Source: First National City Bank, Energy Memo (New York: FNCB), various issues.

TABLE 5.3

Growth in Oil Production, Petroleum Reserves, and Government Oil Revenues, Middle Eastern Countries, 1950–75

| | Annual Compound Rates of Growth | | | | | | | | |
| | Output | | | Reserves | | | Revenues | | |
Country	1950–60	1960–70	1970–75	1950–60	1960–70	1970–75	1950–60	1960–70	1970–75
Algeria	—	18.9	-1.1	18.0	3.4	1.0	—	—	60.0
Iran	4.8	13.8	7.0	17.5	4.8	2.9	12.0	14.4	76.0
Iraq	21.7	4.9	7.6	17.0	2.5	1.4	30.0	7.0	70.5
Kuwait	17.3	5.8	-6.9	19.5	2.1	-2.3	44.2	6.8	53.0
Libya	—	43.9*	-14.9	—	30.9	-1.9	—	55.0*	31.5
Qatar	17.8	8.0	3.5	18.0	5.6	6.4	49.0	8.5	69.4
Saudi Arabia	9.2	11.1	13.5	19.5	10.3	1.4	19.4	13.8	85.0
United Arab Emirates	—	62.1*	16.8	—	12.5*	20.3	—	74.0*	92.0

*Refers to 1962–70.

Sources: BP Statistical Review of the World Oil Industry (London: British Petroleum Company), various issues; American Petroleum Institute, Petroleum Facts and Figures (Washington, D.C.: API, 1971); and "Worldwide Report," Oil and Gas Journal, various issues.

The importance of oil to the economies of the exporting countries may be gauged by the data in Table 5.4. Oil receipts have perennially been the major source of government revenue in most of the OPEC states, and the percentage of government revenue provided by oil exceeded 50 percent in all of the major exporting states by 1975. The share of oil in total exports of these economies shows the lopsidedness of their patterns of development and their heavy dependence on oil as a source of foreign exchange. Even so, oil receipts were not the only benefits to the host countries.

During the concession era, the foreign oil firms had an incentive to upgrade the quality of the local labor supply in order to increase efficiency. They also had an incentive to foster prosperity in the surrounding community as a safeguard against nationalization. Thus, the concessionaires of the Arabian Gulf region provided a variety of services to their host communities, including education, health care, housing, and retirement plans.[8] Adjuncts to the lifting of crude oil included road construction, transport facilities, and harbor development. Once in operation, the services provided by these facilities redounded to the benefit of the larger community.

Firms purchased factors of production on the local markets, thus generating income streams to local labor and entrepreneurs. Demands were created for raw materials and imported goods. In Saudi Arabia, Aramco, a firm with an impressive record for generating external benefits to the community, has operated a technical assistance program for local entrepreneurs since 1947, providing technical advice, feasibility studies, and loans. The firm also has followed a policy of buying supplies locally whenever possible. Although the firm's ultimate purpose may well have been to lower factor costs, the broader social results have been to increase the supply of entrepreneurial talent and to spread economic welfare. The foreign oil firms have served as a linkage to the modern industrial world, through which technology and skills have been transmitted to traditional communities.

The local currency outlays of the firms serve as proximate indicators of their contributions to the host communities. These include expenditures for local goods and labor services used within the enterprise, as well as outlays for projects and programs for the public welfare. Unfortunately, an element of overstatement is included in the data in that expenditures for locally purchased imported goods are included, and these transactions have no effect on the market for

---

tal absorptive capacities, one assumes that the utility of the extra income promised the decision makers by new reserves is presently so low that they have little incentive to attempt to expand reserves.

TABLE 5.4

Petroleum's Contribution to Government Revenue and the Value of Commodity Exports, Middle Eastern Countries, 1967, 1970, 1973, and 1975

Country	Oil Revenue as a Percent of Central Government Revenue				Oil Exports as a Percent of Total Exports			
	1967	1970	1973	1975*	1967	1970	1973	1975*
Algeria	23	21	40	62	74	68	83	91
Iran	49	49	63	85	91	90	92	97
Iraq	57	54	74	85	90	90	92	99
Kuwait	87	83	85	98	97	96	92	91
Libya	77	85	88	90	99	99	99	99
Saudi Arabia	90	88	93	95	89	98	99	99

*Figures for 1975 are the author's provisional estimates.

Sources: International Bank for Reconstruction and Development, World Tables, 1975 (Washington, D. C.: IBRD, 1976); and International Monetary Fund, International Financial Statistics (Washington, D. C.: IMF), various issues.

local resources, other than for the services of middlemen. Even so, the growth of outlays for imported goods implies the development of local commercial institutions and expertise, which, in turn, can be expected to contribute to the economic capability of the larger community.

Among the major oil states as a group, local currency spending by the firms grew steadily throughout the 1960s and into the 1970s. (See Table 5.5.) This expansion was paced by the growth of Aramco's spending in Saudi Arabia, which by the early 1970s exceeded outlays in the other countries by a substantial margin. With 60 percent Saudi ownership, Aramco became a force for planning and implementation beyond its accustomed role in the oil sector, in particular, by taking responsibility for the implementation of the government's gas-gathering and -processing program, as well as the electric power generation program for the Eastern Province. By 1976, local spending by Aramco and its expatriate employees had risen to $1.2 billion.

In conclusion, the relationship between the petroleum enclaves and the host countries is, essentially, one of economic dualism. The modern oil sectors came into being as the result of foreign investment for the exploitation of a natural resource, and the effect was the imposition of vigorous, expanding enclaves upon traditional economies. As new techniques and capital are introduced, established institutions break down and others are altered and transformed. Labor and other factors of production move from the traditional sectors into the modern. In the long run, the new skills acquired in the oil enclaves tend to benefit the traditional sectors by raising their productivity and income. Broadly speaking, the enclaves serve to advance the development of the whole society, as Hirschman linkages are established. Of course, in thinly populated, predominantly desert countries, these effects may be slow in being felt. In any case, the proper role of the state is to facilitate and augment these derived effects by building infrastructure, making wealth transfers, and providing educational and welfare services.

SOVEREIGNTY OVER RESERVES AND
THE PRICE OF OIL

The traditional concessionary arrangements came to an abrupt end in the 1970s, and, as the exporting states took control of their resources, a new era was inaugurated in the international petroleum industry. The consequences of this shift in decision making from the international firms to the producing countries have been profound. It is probable that the terms of trade and the allocation of the world's real and financial resources have been permanently altered by the shift in control of the Middle East's oil reserves.

TABLE 5.5

Local Currency Expenditures by Oil Firms, Middle Eastern Countries, 1960–74
(millions of current U.S. dollars)

Country	1960	1962	1964	1966	1968	1970	1972	1974
Iran	73.7	95.0	88.9	107.7	105.0	124.9	137.0	149.0
Iraq	49.6	47.9	38.4	37.5	52.6	45.6	37.4	33.2
Kuwait	35.0	39.2	51.0	49.0	72.0	116.2	60.4	79.4
Libya	57.7	90.4	131.3	130.8	166.6	209.7	191.8	—
Saudi Arabia	—	76.0	88.0	133.8	—	127.7	261.9	862.0

Sources: Bank Markazi Iran, Annual Report and Balance Sheet (Tehran: BMI), various issues; Statistics and Research Department, Bulletin (Baghdad: Central Bank of Iraq), various issues; Central Bank of Kuwait, Annual Report (Kuwait: CBK), various issues; Economic Research Division, Economic Bulletin (Tripoli: Bank of Libya), various issues; Arabian American Oil Company, A Review of Operations, various annual reports; and International Monetary Fund, Balance of Payments Yearbook (Washington, D.C.: IMF), various issues.

Under the old system, access to inexpensive Middle Eastern oil gave the major oil firms their market power. They were able to administer prices through supply management. With the entry of the independent and state oil firms, it became increasingly difficult for the major commercial firms to control supply. At the same time, the leadership of the oil states was growing increasingly dissatisfied with the economic rewards provided by the existing arrangements.

The nature of the rewards problem can readily be seen by considering Saudi Arabia as a representative producing country. Saudi Arabia returns per barrel during the 1960s are closely correlated ($r = 0.92$) with the per barrel payments to eastern hemisphere governments reported by the First National City Bank. (See Table 5.2.) Thus, Saudi trends are viewed as representative of those of the area at large.

Figure 5.4 shows that while nominal returns grew slowly during the 1960s, inflation in the industrial countries (the oil producers' main trading partners) prevented any real improvement in unit revenues. Real unit revenues were less in 1971 than they were in 1963. In fact, it was not until nominal revenues began to accelerate at an increasing rate after 1971 that real unit returns surpassed their 1955 levels. Although this relative cheapness enabled the international firms to penetrate markets and to convert the industrial world to oil, the producing governments clearly had the incentive to increase their returns per barrel, as they faced world inflation with relatively fixed export prices over which they had no real control.

The overturn of the system began in January 1970, when Libya pressed for higher posted prices for its crude oil. Its bargaining position was inherently strong because of the quality of its oil and its proximity to Europe; moreover, the timing of this move was particularly effective, as Aramco's pipeline to the Mediterranean was closed for repairs. This reduction in the Arabian Gulf oil supply increased Europe's reliance on Libya for Mediterranean oil. In June and August 1970, Libya imposed output restrictions on the firms producing there. * Lacking alternative sources of supply, Occidental Petroleum Company could not withstand this restriction. When, in September, this firm agreed to higher prices, the other independent firms, as well as the

---

*Occidental's output was reduced from 800,000 barrels to 440,000 barrels per day. At the same time, the production ceiling of Standard Oil of California and Texaco (Amoseas) was lowered from 383,000 to 284,000 barrels per day and that of Oasis was reduced to 895,000 from 1,041,000 daily barrels. Mobil's was cut from 260,000 to 222,000 barrels per day. For the group, this represents a ceiling reduction of 26 percent.

FIGURE 5.4

Saudi Arabian Nominal and Real Revenues per Barrel, 1952–76

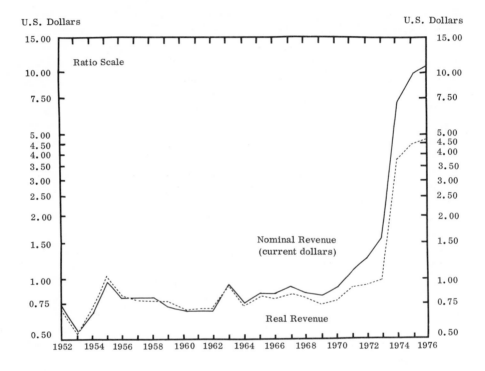

Note: As a first approximation, real revenues per barrel are nominal revenues divided by the IMF's index of the industrial countries' export prices in terms of U.S. dollars (1952 = 100).

Sources: Saudi Arabian Monetary Agency, Annual Report (Jiddah, Kingdom of Saudi Arabia: SAMA), various issues; and International Monetary Fund, International Financial Statistics (Washington, D.C.: IMF), various issues.

major ones, followed suit. The posted price of light crude was raised from $2.23 to $2.53 a barrel, and the tax rate was also increased. Posted prices and tax rates had become negotiable.

After the Libyan settlement, the other exporting states could hardly be expected to forgo increases. The Libyan discovery that output restrictions could produce a seller's market proved to be the hole in the dike. By year's end, the Arabian Gulf exporters, as well as Venezuela and Nigeria, had gained increases in certain posted prices. By threatening supply restrictions, the petroleum-exporting states emerged as the dominant party in negotiations at Tehran early in 1971. In these negotiations, 16 U.S. companies, one Japanese firm, and six West European firms, known as the Group of 23, faced the major Arabian Gulf members of OPEC: Saudi Arabia, Iran, and Iraq. The two main provisions of the final settlement hammered out at Tehran were a uniform increase of 35¢ in posted prices of Arabian Gulf oil, with subsequent increases of 2.5 percent a year to 1975, and an increase in the tax rate to a minimum of 55 percent. The tax-paid cost of oil was thus increased substantially, and further increases were scheduled for years to come. Given the oligopolistic markets faced by the major firms, selling prices of products would be higher, as the additional costs would be passed along to final consumers through markup pricing. Similar increases were arranged subsequently for Mediterranean producers.

These settlements marked a fundamental shift toward the exporting states in the balance of economic power. Further increments to the per barrel dollar revenues of the producing states were provided later through agreements designed to compensate them for losses resulting from dollar devaluation and depreciation. At about the same time, the producer governments increased their efforts toward achieving control of their petroleum resources through outright nationalization, as in Iran, Algeria, Iraq, and Libya, or through participation agreements (phased nationalization), as in Saudi Arabia, Kuwait, and the smaller Arabian Gulf states.

THE OIL WEAPON

The Organization of Arab Petroleum Exporting Countries (OAPEC) was founded in 1968 by Saudi Arabia, Kuwait, and Libya to serve the political and economic interests of those Arab states whose development depended primarily on oil. The underlying assumption was that a small group of Arab producers could behave more cohesively than the more diverse membership of OPEC.* The fourth Arab-

---

*OAPEC's membership subsequently was expanded to include the United Arab Emirates, Algeria, Bahrain, Qatar, Egypt, Syria, and Iraq.

Israeli war (in 1973) served as the occasion for the first successful use of oil as a political weapon. In the second week of the war, the major Arabian Gulf producers announced a 70 percent increase in posted prices. On the following day, OAPEC announced that it would continuously cut exports by 5 percent a month until UN resolutions calling for Israeli withdrawal from occupied Arab territory and the restoration of the rights of the Palestinians
subsequently declared a total embargo on oil to the United States. In addition, an overall cutback in production among Arab producers was set at 25 percent of the September level. In the panic buying that followed, oil sold in the market at over $15 a barrel, and, in December 1973, the Arabian Gulf members of OPEC unilaterally raised the posted price of light crude to $11.65. Thus, the oil weapon consisted of massive price increases, backed by output restrictions. Starting in January 1974, output was gradually restored, and in March the embargo against the United States was suspended. However, the ramifications of the oil weapon's use were more durable.

Tremendous changes have occurred in the prices charged for Middle Eastern oil. (See Table 5.6.) In the three years between February 1, 1971 and January 1, 1974, posted prices, tax-paid costs, and government per barrel revenue increased 500 to 600 percent. In the last quarter of 1973 alone, costs, prices, and revenues increased approximately 300 percent.

The concessionary system in the Middle East was essentially finished by the mid-1970s. The future role of the international firms will probably be one of providing technical services on the basis of commercial contracts for fees and, perhaps, privileged access to oil at prices set by the producing governments. The bilateral monopoly model provides a useful mechanism for appraising the changes of the early 1970s and for outlining future market relations.

Given some level of necessary operating costs and royalty obligation, a rise in posted prices means an increase in notational profit per barrel. This, times the income tax rate (50 or 55 percent), gives an addition to government tax per barrel to the producing firms. Although the profit-sharing formula was referred to as income taxation, it was an excise tax in effect, serving to increase per barrel financial costs and to alter the marginal conditions. In terms of Figure 5.1, the effect of the imposition of higher posted prices is to raise the marginal cost curve of the representative producing firm from MC_0 to MC_1. The firm's preferred output under the new cost conditions becomes OB_1, where marginal revenue product equals the higher marginal cost. The restriction of crude output implies higher prices for oil sold in the open market and for petroleum products, as the tax-paid cost of the marginal barrel rises from B_0C to B_1F.

The traditional role of the international major firms was to ensure continuity of supply at relatively low prices. Through their inter-

TABLE 5.6

The Revolution in Posted Prices, Tax-Paid Costs, and Government Revenues per Barrel, 1971–74
(current U.S. dollars)

Source and Type of Crude	1971 (pre-February 15)			1974 (January 1)		
	Posted Price	Tax-Paid Cost	Government Revenue	Posted Price	Tax-Paid Cost	Government Revenue
Saudi Arabia						
Arabian Light	1.800	1.099	0.989	11.651	7.108	7.008
Arabian Heavy	1.560	0.993	0.843	11.441	6.981	6.881
Iran						
Iranian Light	1.790	1.103	0.983	11.875	7.253	7.133
Iranian Heavy	1.720	1.064	0.944	11.635	7.108	6.988
Kuwait						
Kuwait	1.680	1.018	0.958	11.545	7.026	6.966
Abu Dhabi						
Murban	1.880	1.155	1.005	12.636	7.728	7.578
Iraq						
Basrah	1.720	1.053	0.933	11.672	7.130	7.010
Qatar						
Dukhan	1.930	1.172	1.052	12.414	7.602	7.432

Source: Middle East Economic Survey 17, no. 10 (December 28, 1973).

mediation, direct contact between producing and consuming states was minimal. With the accession of the producing states to control, the buffer function of the firms is disappearing, and producers and consumers increasingly will need to deal with one another directly.

Should the consuming nations organize themselves for collective bargaining, the bilateral monopoly paradigm could be used to consider bargaining situations involving OPEC, as the sellers' bargaining unit and as a bargaining unit representing the consuming nations.* On the basis of purely economic criteria, consumers would wish to purchase relatively large amounts of oil at prices close to the producers' necessary incremental cost of production. OPEC, on the other hand, would favor setting the price near the highest level consumers could be expected to pay for smaller amounts of oil. Thus, the short-term maximizing objectives of the trading blocs are in conflict: negotiation and compromise would lead to a settlement price and output somewhere between these extremes.

Collective boycotts and embargoes, the ultimate weapons implied in bargaining by economic blocs, are hard to maintain in practice. On the demand side, it probably would be difficult for some countries to forgo oil for the sake of other members of the bloc in even a limited boycott of OPEC oil. On the supply side, member states have been unable to reach formal agreement concerning the allocation of market shares. The absence of some sort of prorationing procedure can make it difficult to maintain agreed-upon prices under varying demand conditions. Furthermore, major producers with expensive development programs may not be willing to restrict output to maintain a cartel price. On the other hand, producers with severely limited capital absorptive capacity might be inclined to restrict output, leaving oil in place for the future. Those issues affecting OPEC's cohesiveness are considered further in Chapter 6.

Thirty years ago, the leaders of the Middle Eastern oil states were innocent of the intricacies of the international oil trade. Today, they clearly have mastered the rules of the game. They have learned to take advantage of their long-run, natural strength in newly found bargaining cohesiveness. They have shown themselves to be apt pupils of the international firms. Although the international firms will continue to plan an important role in the Middle East, the governments have emerged as the strategic decision makers on the supply side of the price equation.[9]

---

*In 1974, the International Energy Agency (IEA) emerged as the countercartel of the industrial oil-importing nations. Composed of 19 member countries, IEA's initial policies were oriented toward reducing their collective dependence on imported oil. The IEA is, however, a potential negotiating instrument.

NOTES

1. The factual material cited in the foregoing discussion of concession arrangements in the Middle East was drawn from S. H. Schurr and P. T. Homan, Middle Eastern Oil and the Western World (New York: American Elsevier, 1971), chap. 9; and various issues of Middle East Economic Survey (Beirut).

2. For several good summaries of the economic effects of prorationing, see United States, Senate, Committee on the Judiciary, Government Intervention in the Market Mechanism, pt. 1, Hearing, 91st Cong., 1st sess., March 11–April 2, 1969.

3. George W. Stocking, Middle East Oil (Nashville, Tenn.: Vanderbilt University Press, 1970), p. 420.

4. For an elegant statement of the theory of long-range supply, see M. A. Adelman, The World Petroleum Market (Baltimore: Johns Hopkins University Press, 1972), pp. 13–77.

5. American Petroleum Institute, Petroleum Facts and Figures (Washington, D.C.: API, 1971); and Oil and Gas Journal (Tulsa, Okla.), various issues.

6. Stocking, op. cit., pp. 205–9.

7. Ibid., p. 430.

8. For a good description and analysis of the role of firms in upgrading the quality of labor in the area, see Albert Y. Badre and Simon G. Siksek, Manpower and Oil in Arab Countries (Beirut: Dar al Kitab for Economic Research Institute, American University of Beirut, 1969), especially pp. 52–98.

9. This chapter has benefited from the increasing number of valuable studies available on Middle Eastern oil. In addition to works already cited in the text, these include C. Issawi and M. Yeganah, The Economics of Middle Eastern Oil (New York: Praeger, 1962); F. Rouhani, A History of OPEC (New York: Praeger, 1971); E. E. Penrose, The Large International Firm in Developing Countries (Cambridge, Mass.: The MIT Press, 1969); and A. Mikdashi, The Community of Oil Exporting Countries (Ithaca, N.Y.: Cornell University Press, 1972).

6

OPEC AND
THE PRICE OF OIL

The years 1971–73 represent a turning point in Middle Eastern history. With the accession to control of price and output decision making by the petroleum-exporting countries, the era of cheap energy ended. Henceforth, the probable role of the major international firms will be to act as purveyors of technology and as middlemen in the international distribution system. Economic and political forces now suggest that crude oil prices will tend to be nearer their ceiling than their floor and that world dependence on Middle Eastern energy supplies will increase in the foreseeable future.* The abrupt appearance

*There are effective limits within which the price of oil can vary. The absolute floor price at which oil will be forthcoming in the short run is determined by the necessary cost of the variable factors of production. With an anticipated cost in the 1980s of only 20¢ a barrel (1972 U.S. dollars) in the Gulf region, the floor price of oil from this major OPEC source is low in relation to the prices being realized. On the other hand, the upper limit to oil price movements is set by the necessary cost of close substitutes for OPEC oil.

In the mid 1970s, OPEC oil was still attractive in relation to some of its closest substitutes, according to the following figures for the United States:

Crude Oil	U.S. Dollars per Million British Thermal Units
U.S. regulated (new)	2.00
OPEC	2.41
Shale oil	3.45–4.31
Coal liquefaction	3.45–4.31

of these new conditions was the result of a rare display of collaboration by the Arab states in combining economic, political, and military resources in pursuit of mutually agreed-upon objectives.

CONSEQUENCES OF HIGHER
MIDDLE EASTERN OIL PRICES

A rise in the price of a given quantity of oil, relative to the prices of other internationally traded commodities, means an enlarged flow of resources from the consuming to the exporting nations through trade or capital transactions. If oil is paid for through trade, the output available to the domestic economy of the importing country is reduced by an amount equal in value to the increase in the financial cost of oil. This reduction frees the product to be exported in order to earn foreign exchange to pay for the oil or it permits a reduction of nonoil imports, thus freeing exchange from other uses to pay for the oil. If oil is paid for through capital transactions, the domestic economy's claim on present output is not reduced, but rights to future production are passed to the oil exporters by the exchange of bonds, equities, or real estate. The present economic value of these assets is equal to the promised future income stream discounted by the current rate of return on capital. In sum, oil is exchanged for present or future resources. A higher relative petroleum price means that the consuming states are required to give up larger amounts of present or future resources per unit of oil imported.

In financial terms, the rise in oil revenues represents a significant reallocation of international money.* Balance of payments problems are increased for those countries that have difficulty increasing exports or reducing nonoil imports. Although this effect is a source of strain for the industrialized nations, it also bears heavily on the nonoil states of the Third World, as the industrial nations can more readily pass some of the increased financial costs back to the rest of the world in the form of higher finished goods prices, thereby reducing the real resource cost of oil. Third World nations, on the other hand, typically have lacked market power sufficient to alter their terms of trade, and they usually hold minimal stocks of international monetary reserves.

Not only does more costly oil lead to higher-priced machinery and manufactured goods but also to more expensive fertilizers, plastics, medicines, asphalt paving, synthetic rubber, insecticides, and

_____

*In 1973, the OPEC states held 8 percent of the world's financial reserves; by 1976, their share had risen to 25 percent.

other petroleum derivatives. For nonoil Third World nations, the effects of the new world price relationships could be disastrous without continuous balance-of-payments relief from the petroleum-exporting states, the industrial nations, and the international financial agencies.

On a worldwide basis, other long-range effects of higher relative oil prices are predictable. Wood, peat, and coal will tend to be favored relative to oil, as energy users attempt to offset the latter's higher cost. Thus, the prices of these alternatives must also rise. Techniques of production requiring less commercial energy in relation to human energy will be favored at the margin. As fuel and fertilizer costs are increased, labor-intensive and traditional farming will be strengthened relative to mechanized, modern agriculture. Advantages of large-scale production in modern sectors will be reduced as long-range average cost curves shift upward. In general, real industrial growth among the major oil importers will be slower.

New economies of urban scale will be reduced, ceteris paribus, thus contributing to a potential lessening of urban growth rates. Modern military operations, in general, will be more costly. Transportation costs will rise, and energy-intensive manufactured products will become more costly relative to primary products and services. Market forces will orient invention and innovation toward the development of new energy sources: shale oil, coal liquefaction and gasification, hydro- and geothermal electricity, and nuclear and solar energy. Finally, the success of OPEC will spur other primary exporting nations to attempt to raise other basic resource prices through supply restrictions. If successful, their efforts could have a profound effect on the terms of trade between the major economic blocs of nations.*

The initial impact of the oil price explosion on the OPEC nations was staggering. Combined oil revenues accruing to OPEC govern-

---

*The effects of the oil price rise on the terms of trade (an index of export prices divided by an index of import prices) can be gauged by comparing the Middle East with other world regions:

Region	UN Terms of Trade Indexes (1970 = 100)		
	1973	1974	1975
Asian Middle East	124	312	275
North America	96	88	89
Europe	99	87	93
Africa	113	154	131
Other Asia	100	94	86

ments rose from $22.5 billion in 1973 to $91.9 billion in 1974, an increase of 308 percent, while at the same time, their petroleum exports declined about 2.5 percent. Had 1974 exports continued to generate average unit revenue at the 1973 rate, the oil revenues accruing to the OPEC governments in 1974 would have been only $21.9 billion. Thus, the price-induced income transfer from the rest of the world to the OPEC countries was about $70 billion. Although it was little more than 1 percent of 1974 world GNP, this extra income represented nearly 40 percent of the OPEC members' GNP at that time.

The immediate concern, as this transfer continued, was that the OPEC countries would not be able to increase their imports fast enough to recycle these extra revenues back into the channels of world trade and that the resulting leakage of funds would stifle commerce and lead to world depression. Coming as it did at a time of Western monetary restraint, OPEC price increases did contribute to the world recession of 1974-75, but the more dire consequences predicted did not arise. In general, OPEC's collective capacity for importing has been greater than forecast, and the international banking system has been able to channel surplus funds into the hands of borrowers, many of whom suddenly needed financing to pay for oil and higher-priced industrial goods. The question of equity in the distribution of the resulting debt burden between richer and poorer nations is a far more ominous world problem than is the absolute size of OPEC surpluses.

While OPEC government oil revenue growth increased sharply in 1974 and then slowed at a higher level, imports continued to grow fairly steadily until 1976, when port and transportation bottlenecks slowed their inflow. Under these combined influences, the mercurial OPEC surplus spurted to $67 billion, but then declined abruptly.* With increases in port capacities and improvement in other forms of infrastructure, the surplus of most exporting countries can be expected to continue to decline.

The OPEC surplus is more precisely an Arabian Gulf surplus. At mid-decade, approximately half of the OPEC surplus accrued to Saudi Arabia alone, and, when the United Arab Emirates, Kuwait, and Qatar are included, the Gulf states accounted for more than 80

---

*An OPEC member's investable surplus is its current international payments balance after transfers have been made to foreigners. By 1976, about 35 percent of the cumulative surplus had been placed in Eurocurrency bank deposits, with another 28 percent in U.S. assets. The remaining third was divided between investments in Great Britain, contributions to the international agencies, grants and loans to individual countries, and miscellaneous net flows.

percent. Their large oil reserves, their small populations, and
their limited production possibilities outside of the petroleum sector
imply a tendency to accumulate surpluses not to be found among the
larger OPEC states, which have greater development needs and inherently higher propensities to import. In the long run, the world
price of oil will be strongly influenced by the way in which Saudi
Arabia resolves its output dilemma. Meeting world oil demand at
fairly stable relative prices implies rapid output growth, accelerated
oil depletion, and a greater investable surplus management problem.
But, on the other hand, restriction of output to levels needed for internal development suggests chronic excess demand conditions, rising relative oil prices, and increasing tension between the exporting
states and the consuming states.

OPEC'S MARKET POWER

At any moment in time, society is employing some stock of
energy-utilizing capital. Petroleum-dependent equipment's share of
this stock is influenced by the relative prices of alternative energy
sources. When the long-term prices of petroleum products are low
relative to those of substitutes, the proportion of the energy-using
equipment dependent on oil will tend to be large. Once a society's
stock of energy-using equipment has become dependent on petroleum
products, it is probably cheaper to pay substantially higher prices
for oil than to forgo the use of the equipment. Thus, in the short run,
there is little latitude at the margin for the substitution of alternatives
for petroleum. As the price explosion of 1973-74 confirms, the
world's short-term petroleum demand is relatively inelastic, but, in
the long run, this is less likely to be the case. Given time, energy-
saving technology can be devised and embodied in new capital formation; alternative energy sources can be developed, and new equipment
can be designed. In the long run, the higher the price of OPEC oil,
the more likely it is that new alternatives will be developed and that
importers will find ways to economize on the use of OPEC oil.

In recent years, the major industrial countries and the world
at large have become increasingly dependent on oil as an energy
source. (See Table 6.1.) When natural gas is included, the two associated products together account for nearly two-thirds of the world's
energy supply. Reliance on oil and gas among the developed market
economies is substantially higher. OPEC's market strength is readily
apparent when its control of supply is weighed against the world's
present oil dependence. (See Table 6.2.) At mid-decade, the two
largest national producers, the USSR and the United States, together
accounted for a third of the world's crude oil production but held only

TABLE 6.1

Energy Sources, 1967 and 1976
(percent)

| | Resource Shares in Total Energy Supply | | | |
	Oil	Natural Gas	Solid Fuel	Hydro/ Nuclear
United States				
1967	40.8	33.4	21.6	4.2
1976	45.3	28.4	19.3	7.0
Western Europe				
1967	50.6	3.2	36.0	10.2
1976	56.2	13.3	20.7	9.8
Japan				
1967	62.5	1.0	26.8	9.7
1976	71.3	3.1	16.9	8.7
USSR				
1967	29.1	20.1	47.5	3.3
1976	35.5	23.6	36.2	4.7
World				
1967	39.8	17.0	37.0	6.2
1976	44.8	17.8	30.1	7.3

Source: BP Statistical Review of the World Oil Industry 1976 (London: British Petroleum Company, 1977).

18 percent of the world's proved reserves; OPEC members produced over half the world's current oil supply but held among them two-thirds of the world's reserves. As over 85 percent of OPEC's reserves and 80 percent of its production are in the Middle East, the organization's continued market power depends on the compliance of these members.

Europe and Japan rely on the area for more than three-quarters of their oil, and the dependence of the United States, the world's largest consumer, has greatly increased in the past decade. (See Table 6.3.) One of the main factors behind OPEC's rising influence is the decline of U.S. reserve capacity and its increasing dependence on imported oil. It is no longer possible for the United States to compensate for a Middle Eastern supply interruption by increasing its domestic output, as it did in 1956 and 1967; in 1973, there was no surplus capacity to compensate for the Arab oil embargo. Barring sizable but un-

TABLE 6.2

Relative Size of OPEC and Other Oil Producers, 1976
(percent)

	Output	Proved Reserves	Reserves/Output Ratio
Shares in world oil			
United States	15.7	5.2	9.3
USSR	17.6	13.0	21.4
Middle East	43.1	60.6	43.6
OPEC*	52.2	66.6	39.9
Shares in OPEC oil			
Iran	19.2	15.8	29.2
Saudi Arabia	28.3	28.4	35.4
Saudi Arabia with Kuwait, Qatar, and the United Arab Emirates	43.2	55.3	45.2

*Includes Algeria, Ecuador, Gabon, Indonesia, Iran, Iraq, Kuwait, Libya, Nigeria, Qatar, Saudi Arabia, the United Arab Emirates, and Venezuela.

Sources: "Worldwide Report," Oil and Gas Journal 74, no. 52 (December 27, 1976); and BP Statistical Review of the World Oil Industry, 1976 (London: British Petroleum Company, 1977).

likely U.S. discoveries, its relatively low reserves/output ratio suggests that the reliance of the United States on imported oil will grow.

These considerations imply continued dependence on OPEC in the foreseeable future. A substantial reduction in the world's dependence on the OPEC members will involve a much greater reliance on solid fuels and development of the more exotic alternative sources, as well as on finding and developing non-OPEC oil reserves. Movement in these directions by the consuming nations will be slow, so that OPEC will probably remain a key factor in the world energy situation for many years to come.

INSIDE OPEC

In terms of its institutional structure, OPEC policy decisions are made by the Conference, a body composed of representatives of

TABLE 6.3

World Oil Consumption and Imports, 1967 and 1976

	Oil Consumption (millions of tons)	Shares in World Oil Consumption (percent)	Net Imports as a Percentage of Consumption	Middle Eastern Oil as a Percentage of Consumption*
United States				
1967	595.8	33.7	19.3	2.1
1976	822.4	28.6	42.9	16.8
Western Europe				
1967	458.1	25.9	99.9	74.3
1976	706.4	24.5	96.5	77.4
Japan				
1967	122.9	6.9	97.6	83.0
1976	253.8	8.8	100.0	78.2
USSR, Eastern Europe, and People's Republic of China				
1967	260.7	14.7	-20.7	—
1976	536.0	18.6	-17.4	—

*Includes North Africa.

Source: BP Statistical Review of the World Oil Industry (London: British Petroleum Company), 1967 and 1976 issues.

the member countries.* As the agency ultimately responsible for policy, the Conference meets at least twice yearly to consider the recommendations of the organization's board of governors. The Conference's policy resolutions, which include the setting of oil prices for the next six months, require the unanimity of its members. Before 1973, the Conference was absorbed with developing strategies to increase the member countries' shares in the profits of the oil firms, but with the governments' accession to control, it shouldered responsibility for commercial decisions that directly affected the world oil market, both currently and in the future. For want of a better descriptive title, OPEC may be referred to as a cartel. However, national trading organizations are different from those of ordinary business in that their behavior will almost inevitably be influenced by political as well as economic considerations.

A "perfect" business cartel seeks to maximize the joint profits of its members by allocating production quotas among them in order to equate the cartel's marginal cost with its marginal revenue. The cartel behaves, in effect, as a multiplant monopoly firm. Profits are distributed among the producing members according to some formula agreed upon in advance. This mode of operation is achieved at the expense of the decision-making prerogatives of the participants.

In practice, complete surrender of price and output responsibility to a central authority is unlikely, and quotas and profit shares are determined by the give and take of negotiation. Under this procedure, however, cartel profits will probably not be maximized. A still less demanding procedure would be for the cartel to set prices, allowing the members to sell all they can at these official prices. All that is required here is that no producer attempt to sell below cartel prices and that the rates of production of individual members are, in effect, left to the demands of the clientele. The OPEC process resembles this less formal collusive arrangement.

OPEC is presently a loose confederation of oil-producing states, held together by the common conviction that each is economically and politically better off through association than it would be otherwise.

---

*Other agencies within OPEC include the board of governors, the Economic Commission, and the secretariat. The governors are responsible for the organization's budget and for the implementation of the resolutions of the Conference. The secretariat is the actual administrative branch of OPEC; run by professionals, it conducts the organization's day-to-day affairs. Legal, engineering, and economic research and analysis are all within its purview. The Economic Commission is a representative agency that meets twice yearly to oversee the work of the secretariat.

As a means to economic betterment, its members share a common interest in achieving and maintaining petroleum prices that are high in relation to the prices they must pay for imported goods. OPEC's success in this regard served to build confidence in its economic value, and its cohesiveness was further strengthened by its tangible political worth. Its member states share new influence and prestige in the non-Western world, derived from being the first primary producers to alter their terms of trade substantially vis-à-vis the industrial nations through collective action. Even though the immediate effect was higher energy and fertilizer costs, the Third World at large, officially, has supported OPEC because its success hints at wealth redistribution in favor of the exporters of primary products.

The flexibility of OPEC's operational process is reflected in its procedures for price and output determination. Under current arrangements, the price of Saudi Arabian light oil serves as the reference value for the pricing of other oils. Relative to that of Arabian light oil, other OPEC prices are supposed to reflect not only gravity differences but also differential site and quality advantages among alternative sources of supply. Under this procedure, Libyan light crude, for example, would be expected to sell at a premium because of its proximity to Europe and its low sulfur content. As long as administered price differentials accurately measure the economic advantages offered by alternative supplies, established market shares should be maintained, and price-induced shifts in demands for alternative supplies should be eliminated. Given such a set of OPEC prices, members are free to sell as much output as they can. In principle, prices are set at levels that are neutral as far as market shares are concerned, with the rate of output left to be determined by the demands of the buyers.

There are inherent problems implied by these arrangements. The essential difficulty is that OPEC prices need not be net revenue maximizing prices. (See the Appendix.) When the difference between a member's OPEC price and its optimum price is substantial, the incentive to break ranks and follow independent policies can weaken OPEC's cohesiveness. The potential for disharmony is increased by the economic and political diversity of its membership.

Within OPEC, a wide variety of general economic conditions are represented. The thinly populated capital surplus states of the Gulf could meet their development needs with lower rates of oil production than they were actually providing in the mid-1970s. Saudi Arabia, for instance, would have been amply served by producing at about half of its 11.9 million daily barrel capacity. On the other hand, such populous countries as Algeria, Iran, Nigeria, and Indonesia can fully utilize their oil revenues and, therefore, are sensitive to lost income opportunities. Furthermore, political differences are also reflected in the Conference. With its use as a weapon in 1973, oil acquired a unique political character, but the OPEC members are not in agreement as to how it should be employed in the future. Radical states, such as Iraq, Libya, and Algeria, are not as sensitive to the negative effects of additional price increases on the oil-dependent industrial nations of the West as are the smaller and more traditional states of the Gulf. Saudi Arabia, in particular, is aware that its national security and prosperity are inextricably bound up with that of the major consuming states. As a consequence, it has consistently played a moderating role in Conference debates. These differences in situation and policy add to the chance of disagreement within OPEC when demand shifts among sources of supply abruptly create gaps between optimum and official prices.

The demand curves faced by individual producing states are influenced not just by the overall world demand for oil but by the composition of demand, as well as by supply and demand forces in related markets. Oil is not homogeneous but is subject to quality variations. As already noted, Saudi light crude serves as the reference value for other oils, and other OPEC prices relative to it are structured to reflect gravity, site, and other quality differences. As the world tanker spot market is almost perfectly competitive, variations in the overall demand for oil are instantly reflected in freight rates. A fall in world oil demand lowers shipping costs and encourages oil companies to purchase oil from more distant markets. A rise in oil demand has the opposite effect. Variations in world demand also influences the demand for the services of desulfurization plants. Excess capacity in these plants discourages the purchase of premium low-sulfur crudes.

These factors contributed to an inequitable distribution of the burden among the organization's members when OPEC exports declined in the 1974 recession: exports from Saudi Arabia, Iran, the United Arab Emirates, Nigeria, and Indonesia actually increased, while those of Kuwait, Algeria, and Libya declined. The resulting reallocation of market shares was caused primarily by the failure of

---

*The reasons behind Saudi Arabia's policy of price moderation are complex. A small anticommunist country of modest military capability, Saudi Arabia recognizes that its security ultimately depends on Western strength. It has no desire to undermine Western prosperity by accelerating the wealth transfer. Second, oil and politics are now inextricably bound together. Saudi Arabia expects U.S. contributions to Middle Eastern peace as a quid pro quo. Finally, it is mindful of the contribution expensive oil makes to the debt burdens of the nonoil Third World countries.

OPEC's administered price structure to respond adequately to reces-
sion-induced shifts in demand among alternative sources of supply.

The decline in world industrial production and petroleum consumption produced excess capacity in desulfurization plants and a
decline in tanker freight rates. The result was a shift in demand toward longer haul and higher sulfur crudes. The site and quality advantages of Libyan crude, for example, were lowered in relation to
their administered supply prices. As short-haul crudes became over-
priced, long-haul crudes became cheaper in terms of delivered prices.
Similarly, crudes that carried a low sulfur premium tended to lose
their attractiveness.

Although some output reductions in 1974 were primarily attrib-
utable to deliberate conservation measures, as in Kuwait, the redistribution of market shares in the recession period was largely unin-
tended and thus presented OPEC with an internal equity problem.
With the continuation of the recession into 1975, the decline in demand
affected all OPEC members. To defend the benchmark price, Saudi
Arabian production was cut back, and in the second quarter of 1975,
little more than 50 percent of its full capacity was being utilized.

With recovery of world demand, the other side of the problem
was revealed, as rising optimum prices produced a serious division
with OPEC. Unable to reach agreement on the next year's prices,
the Conference broke ranks at the Doha conference of December 1976.
Eleven members reached agreement on a 10 percent increase for the
first six months, to be followed by an additional 5 percent increase
for the second half of 1977. Saudi Arabia and the United Arab Emirates, on the other hand, opposed an increase of this size and agreed
to mark up prices by 5 percent for the year. The emergence of this
two-tier pricing system represented OPEC's first public split on
pricing policy.

By utilizing its ample reserve capacity, Saudi Arabia's strategy
was to satisfy the demand its lower prices attracted, increase sales
at the expense of its opponents, and thus force a compromise on pricing. In practice, this strategy put Saudi Arabia in direct conflict
with Iran, Iraq, and Kuwait, whose oil is similar in quality and location. Although Saudi Arabian output expansion was slowed by bad
weather and temporary bottlenecks, it was achieving its purposes by
midyear. Saudi Arabia's share of OPEC production rose from 29
percent in January to 32 percent in June, while the share of the leading antagonist, Iran, declined from 18 to 17 percent. The 11 agreed
in July to forgo their intended 5 percent additional increase, while
Saudi Arabia and the United Arab Emirates increased their prices
another 5 percent in order to restore a unified price structure. In
pursuing this policy, Saudi Arabia showed it was willing to risk the
breakup of OPEC and strain its relations with Iran to achieve its pur-

poses.* By doing so, it emerged as first among equals and, clearly, the dominant OPEC member.

Lacking agreement on some form of prorationing, OPEC's process of pricing is becoming increasingly dependent on the market leadership of Saudi Arabia, whose large inventory of oil in place enables it to maintain a substantial reserve capacity. By expanding or contracting its own output, it can proximately maintain the short-run price structure it prefers. When world demand for OPEC oil is strong and spot prices of the smaller producers are rising, an expansion of Saudi Arabian output at a relatively lower price would divert demand from the smaller producers to it, lower their optimum prices, and, thus, reduce their incentive to raise their official prices. When world demand is weak and discounts are being offered by the smaller producers, a decrease in Saudi Arabian output would shift demand to them, bolster optimum prices, and lessen their desire to cut prices. By providing the discipline OPEC otherwise is lacking, Saudi Arabia can maintain orderly markets. Although the market shares of the OPEC members will probably be more stable than they would without effective Saudi Arabian leadership, their variability remains an unresolved problem within OPEC.

PRODUCERS AND CONSUMERS

Long-term oil market conditions depend on such imponderables as the rate of the world's industrial growth and the extent to which non-OPEC energy resources are developed, as well as on the development of the OPEC supply. Particularly important factors influencing supply conditions are the incentives provided by governments to encourage the development of new energy resources, the possible decline of the USSR as a net exporter of oil, and Saudi Arabia's willingness to expand capacity and production.

Numerous studies on the energy problem have been conducted since 1973 by reputable institutions and research groups. Most agree that during the next two decades, Saudi Arabia will be called upon to play a unique role in meeting the world's energy needs.† If, for ex-

---

*With the establishment of the two-tier price system, the Shah of Iran publicly asserted that he viewed an increase in production by Saudi Arabia at the expense of those who needed the income as an act of aggression.

†This includes work by the Central Intelligence Agency, the OECD, Exxon, and the World Alternative Energy Strategy (sponsored by the Massachusetts Institute of Technology).

ample, the total quantity of oil demanded were to grow at only 3 percent a year, world production would have to rise from 59 million daily barrels in 1976 to more than 76 million by 1985 to satisfy that demand. After allowing for newly developed oil from the North Sea, Alaska, and Mexico and for declining production in Iran, Kuwait, and Venezuela, prevailing opinion suggests that Saudi Arabia will have to export at least 16 million barrels a day if oil prices are to be kept fairly stable in relation to other commodity prices. To double capacity and output, approximately, in less than a decade presents formidable developmental and administrative problems, and it is probable that Saudi Arabia will find its indispensibility a heavy burden in these respects.

Assuming that revenues per barrel rise no faster than the rate of world inflation, say, 4 percent a year, by 1985, Saudi Arabian oil revenues would be $92 billion if it were exporting then at the rate of 16 million barrels a day. With its limited production possibilities, aside from the oil and petrochemical sectors, Saudi Arabia probably would need to produce 6 million to 8 million barrels a day for the purposes of internal development. With oil gradually growing more scarce, Saudi Arabia may find little or no economic incentive to supply the additional barrels. In fact, with the prospect of rising oil prices generating a positive expected rate of return on oil in place, it might very well prefer a practice conservation. Should Saudi Arabia follow a policy of slow output growth, the price of oil could rise to $30 to $40 a barrel in the 1980s. As an inducement to produce, Saudi Arabia and other similarly situated exporters will need access to capital markets offering attractive rates of return at fairly low risk. As these requirements can only be met in the West, accommodation between producers and consumers is needed.

In retrospect, there are several areas of mutual interest in which both consumers and producers can benefit from collaboration. Since new oil will have to come from increasingly expensive sources, the era of cheap fossil energy would sooner or later have had to end. OPEC's actions in 1973 simply telescoped the process. Although the major firms could have eased and elongated the transition, high-priced energy would have come eventually. As it is, the precipitous rise in prices made investment in previously uneconomic alternatives worthwhile. Plans for the development of coal, shale, offshore oil, and nuclear resources are now based on the assumed permanence of OPEC prices. Should these prices suddenly fall, new investments in alternative energy sources would be uneconomic, and capital would be wasted. Thus, with every passing year, the industrial oil-importing nations will have an increasing interest in the continuation of OPEC in its present guise. The reserve strength of Saudi Arabia underpins this continuity.

As Saudi Arabian supplies become ever more important to the consuming nations, the Saudi Arabian dilemma will become more acute. As already noted, capacity and output growth will be necessary to keep markets orderly and to moderate the rise in oil prices relative to other commodities. Under these circumstances, Saudi Arabia and other Gulf producers will need secure and profitable outlets for their surplus capital, while the major consumers will need capital inflows to balance their oil-derived current payments deficits.

It may well be that the net effect of higher oil prices will be a reallocation of resources that strengthens the relative world positions of the major industrial economies. Among these economies, higher energy costs will tend to dampen present real consumption, but, at the same time, purchases of industrial equipment and manufactured goods by the oil exporters and their aid recipients should stimulate the export sectors of industry, raising rates of return on capital there and, thus, attracting investable resources from abroad. In real terms, the industrial countries would be trading manufactured goods and high technology products for capital and petroleum. To the extent that this process quickens rates of capital formation and technological progress, the adverse effects of more expensive energy could be offset in the long run. Thus, there is a substantial degree of complementarity in the situation, as it is evolving in the 1970s, and a potential for mutual gain in the long run. The evolving special relationship between the United States and Saudi Arabia apparently is based on a recognition of this, as are the commercial policies of West Germany, France, and Japan.* Through bilateral arrangements, the major producers and consumers are negotiating the future oil supply on a piecemeal basis.

Should time confirm these relationships, it will be imperative that Third World producers lacking in market power not become the "odd men out," permanently relegated to the position of suppliers of raw materials to the affluent world of industrial and oil-producing countries. Through policies of unrestricted trade and development assistance, the affluent states can continue to foster the development and diversification of the Third World economies. Furthermore, it is particularly important that the oil states do not allow this unique opportunity for substantial regional development to slip away unrealized before oil reserves are depleted.

---

*According to press reports, the United States is providing contributions to Saudi Arabian security and Middle Eastern peace: outlets for Saudi Arabian capital through investment in new sources of energy, advanced technology, and other attractive outlets in the United States, and an enlarged Saudi Arabian role in the World Bank and the IMF. This would be in exchange for the satisfaction of the future oil needs of the United States at agreed-upon prices secured through Saudi Arabian leverage within OPEC.

7

STRUCTURAL CHANGE

There is a lack of symmetry in the relationship between balanced economic development and per capita income. While it is true that no well-balanced, modern economies have low per capita incomes, rudimentary and essentially traditional societies may or may not have high incomes. Fortuitous mineral wealth can produce inordinately high incomes, but when such special advantages are absent, low income means that capital formation will be small, and economic opportunities will be limited to the traditional sectors.

Malthus observed that among the wealthier nations there is a smaller proportion of people employed in agriculture than in the poorer nations. In the former, a greater proportion is to be found employed in the production of conveniences and luxuries.[1] This implies that rising output is associated with a shift of population from the agricultural sector into other sectors of the economy. Referring to 1820 England, Malthus noted that the ratio of persons engaged in commerce and nonagricultural activities to those in agriculture was as high as three to two.[2] Thus, about 40 percent of the labor force was employed in agriculture at that time. Today, only about 3 percent of the economically active population is employed in that sector.

Inquiry along these lines has been extended much further. Research confirms that, as development proceeds, agriculture's share in the labor force tends to decline, while that of industry increases. Eventually, the labor force share of the industrial sector reaches some upper limit and thereafter declines, as the share of the services sector continues to grow. Income elasticities of demand for the sectoral products of industry and services tend to be much higher than for primary products. As incomes grow, demands for final goods and factors of production shift away from agriculture toward secondary and tertiary sectors. Higher per worker productivity and wages

in the expanding sectors encourage the migration of labor from the
primary sector. Under these circumstances, such labor transfers
serve to increase national income and to sustain the process of
structural change.[3]

Recently, the scope of this analysis has been broadened to include alterations in society beyond changes in industrial structure.
For example, Kuznets observes that changes occur in the shares of
domestic and foreign supplies, in the relation between births and
deaths, in urban-rural proportions, and in the rate of change in technology and its utilization in the production process.[4] These changes
imply alterations in other social institutions, such as the family,
patterns of education, and styles of life in general. Such transfor-
mations are implied by the term modernization.

INDUSTRIAL STRUCTURE

Estimates of agriculture, industry, and services sectoral shares
in GDP reveal distinct differences between the major petroleum producers and the other states of the area. (See Table 7.1.) In general,
the sectoral shares for agriculture and services tend to be smaller in
the oil states than in the nonoil states. Industry sectoral shares are
larger in the oil states because petroleum sector value added is
counted as industrial production. The unusually large sectoral shares
for services found in the nonoil states reflect the area's traditional
emphasis on trade and commercial activity, while the lack of industrial alternatives means that agriculture remains an important source
of income in these countries.

Through time, some basic tendencies in the patterns of change
can be discerned: only in Iraq, Egypt, and South Yemen has the long-
run relative contribution of agriculture failed to decline; and only in
Iraq, South Yemen, and the Sudan has the industry sector share failed
to rise. The general characteristics of the area are the declining
relative importance of agriculture as a source of income and the rising importance of industry.

Among both the oil states and the others, agriculture's share
in product is negatively correlated with 1974 per capita income,
while industry's share is positively correlated. (See Table 7.2.)
Thus, on a cross-country basis in the Middle East, as in the world at
large, rising per capita incomes are associated with declining sector
shares for agriculture and rising sector shares for industry.

These relationships, however, are not particularly close, especially among the oil states. This reflects one of the peculiarities of
oil-based growth, which is that rapidly increasing oil rents can raise
per capita income to high levels without concomitant industrialization
having taken place.

TABLE 7.1

Sectoral Shares in GDP, Middle Eastern Countries, 1960s and 1970s[a]

	Percentage Shares by Sector of Production					
	Early 1960s			Early 1970s		
	Agriculture[b]	Industry[c]	Services[d]	Agriculture[b]	Industry[c]	Services[d]
Major oil states						
Algeria	21.0	22.0	57.0	8.0	44.0	48.0
Iran	29.0	33.0	38.0	12.0	59.0	29.0
Iraq	17.0	52.0	31.0	18.0	46.0	36.0
Kuwait	0.4	72.5	27.1	0.3	72.6	27.1
Libya	10.0	37.0	53.0	3.0	68.0	29.0
Saudi Arabia	9.0	61.0	30.0	3.0	79.0	18.0
Other states						
Bahrain	—	—	—	1.0	75.0	24.0
Egypt	30.0	24.0	46.0	31.0	27.0	42.0
Israel	11.0	32.0	57.0	6.0	37.0	57.0
Jordan	16.0	14.0	70.0	14.0	21.0	65.0
Lebanon	12.0	20.0	68.0	9.0	21.0	70.0
Morocco	30.0	23.0	47.0	24.0	27.0	49.0
Southern Yemen	17.0	15.0	68.0	21.0	11.0	68.0
Sudan	58.0	15.0	27.0	38.0	15.0	47.0
Syria	25.0	21.0	54.0	17.0	23.0	60.0
Tunisia	25.0	25.0	50.0	19.0	27.0	54.0
Turkey	40.0	23.0	37.0	27.0	31.0	42.0

[a]GDP at factor cost.

[b]Includes farming, forestry, hunting, and fishing.

[c]Includes mining and quarrying, manufacturing, construction, and public utilities (electricity, gas, water, and sanitary services).

[d]Includes wholesale and retail trade, transport, storage, communications, finance, public administration, and personal services.

Sources: International Bank for Reconstruction and Development, World Tables (Washington, D.C.: IBRD), 1971 and 1975 issues; and United Nations, Yearbook of National Accounts Statistics (New York: United Nations), various issues.

TABLE 7.2

Correlation between 1974 per Capita Incomes and Contemporary Sectoral Shares,
Middle Eastern Countries

States	r
Correlation between incomes and shares in GDP	
Major oil states	
Agriculture sector[a]	−0.683
Industry sector[b]	0.594
Services sector[c]	−0.391
Other states	
Agriculture sector[a]	−0.731
Industry sector[b]	0.658
Services sector[c]	−0.227
Correlation between incomes and shares in the labor force	
Major oil states	
Agriculture sector[a]	−0.923
Industry sector[b]	0.775
Services sector[c]	0.961
Other states	
Agriculture sector[a]	−0.814
Industry sector[b]	0.869
Services sector[c]	0.762

[a]Includes farming, forestry, hunting, and fishing.
[b]Includes mining and quarrying, manufacturing, construction, and public utilities (electricity, gas, water, and sanitary services).
[c]Includes wholesale and retail trade, transport, storage, communications, finance, public administration, and personal services.

Sources: International Bank for Reconstruction and Development, World Tables (Washington, D.C.: IBRD), 1971 and 1975 issues; United Nations, Yearbook of National Accounts Statistics (New York: United Nations), various issues; International Labour Organization, Year Book of Labour Statistics, 1974 (Geneva: ILO, 1974); Central Planning Organization, Kingdom of Saudi Arabia, Development Plan 1390 A.H. (Riyadh: Government of Saudi Arabia, 1970); United States–Saudi Arabian Joint Commission on Economic Cooperation, Summary of Saudi Arabian Five Year Development Plan, 1975–1980 (Washington, D.C.: Department of the Treasury, 1975); General Statistical Organization, Republic of Iraq, Annual Abstract of Statistics (Baghdad: Ministry of Planning), various issues; United Nations, Statistical Yearbook, 1974 (New York: United Nations, 1975); International Bank for Reconstruction and Development, World Bank Atlas, 1975 (Washington, D.C.: IBRD, 1975); Food and Agricultural Organization of the United Nations, Production Yearbook, 1974 (Rome, FAO, 1975); and Economic Commission for Africa, Summaries of Economic Data (Addis Ababa, Ethiopia: ECA), various issues.

This is somewhat at odds with the conclusions of Kuznets.[5] In studying 1958 data for 57 countries, both developed and developing but excluding the mineral-rich countries, he found that variations in the shares of the agriculture and industry sectors were closely associated with variations in per capita income. In considering the services sector, Kuznets found the worldwide relation between per capita income and the services sector to be positive, although weak. In the Middle East, these coefficients are low and negative.

Changes in sectoral shares in the value of production imply alterations in the allocation of resources and the structure of demand for productive factors, including labor. Changes in shares in the labor force normally accompany changes in sectoral shares in output. In general, the agriculture sector's share in the labor force has fallen in recent years, while the shares of the industry and services sectors have risen. (See Table 7.3.)

As in the case of shares in product, there are differences between the oil-producing and nonoil-producing states in the distribution of sectoral shares in the labor force. In general, agriculture's share in labor tends to be higher in the nonoil states than in the oil states. Differences in industry and services sector shares are less obvious, but the sectoral shares in labor are somewhat lower on the average in the nonoil states. In both oil and nonoil states, the agriculture sectoral share in the labor force is strongly and negatively correlated with per capita income, while the shares of the industry and services sectors are positively correlated with income. (See Table 7.2.) These findings conform fairly well to the results of studies of these relationships in other parts of the world, but it should be remembered that income and social development need not be closely related in the contemporary Middle East.

Differences in sectoral shares in production and the labor force mean differences in output per worker. Employing Kuznets's method, a sector's share in production divided by its share in the labor force yields that sector's output per worker, expressed as a ratio to nationwide product per worker.* Relative productivities measured on this basis are presented in Table 7.4, where, for example, Algeria's 1960 agriculture sector share in output (21.0 in Table 7.1) divided by

---

$$\frac{^*Ya}{Yt} \div \frac{La}{Lt} = \frac{Ya}{Yt} \times \frac{Lt}{La} = \frac{Ya}{La} \times \frac{Lt}{Yt} = \frac{Ya}{La} : \frac{Yt}{Lt}$$

where Ya and Yt represent the agriculture sector's output and the output of the total economy, respectively; La is the amount of labor employed in that sector; and Lt is the total labor force (see Simon Kuznets, Economic Growth of Nations [Cambridge, Mass.: Harvard University Press, 1971], p. 208).

TABLE 7.3

Sectoral Shares in the Labor Force, Middle Eastern Countries, 1960s and 1970s

| | Percentage Shares by Sector of Production | | | | | |
| | Early 1960s | | | Early 1970s | | |
Country	Agriculture[a]	Industry[b]	Services[c]	Agriculture[a]	Industry[b]	Services[c]
Major oil states						
Algeria	74	5	21	56	13	31
Iran	55	23	22	41	24	35
Iraq	49	11	40	56	10	34
Kuwait	1	34	65	2	34	64
Libya	37	19	44	30	22	48
Saudi Arabia	46	18	36	28	28	44
Other states						
Bahrain	—	—	—	7	34	59
Egypt	57	12	31	49	16	35
Israel	17	35	48	9	34	57
Jordan	35	26	39	29	71	
Lebanon	27	73		19	24	57
Morocco	56	11	33	50	15	35
Southern Yemen	71	15	14	62	38	
Sudan	86	6	8	89	3	8
Syria	47	17	36	54	18	28
Tunisia	69	18	13	53	19	28
Turkey	71	12	17	67	12	21

[a]Includes farming, forestry, hunting, and fishing.

[b]Includes mining and quarrying, manufacturing, construction, and public utilities (electricity, gas, water, and sanitary services).

[c]Includes wholesale and retail trade, transport, storage, communications, finance, public administration, and personal services.

Sources: International Bank for Reconstruction and Development, World Tables (Washington, D. C.: IBRD), 1971 and 1975 issues; and International Labour Organization, Year Book of Labour Statistics, 1974 (Geneva: ILO, 1974). Estimates of sectoral shares for Saudi Arabia are based on information found in Central Planning Organization, Development Plan 1390 A. H. (Riyadh: Government of Saudi Arabia, 1970); and United States–Saudi Arabian Joint Commission on Economic Cooperation, Summary of Saudi Arabian Five Year Development Plan, 1975–1980 (Washington, D. C.: Department of the Treasury, 1975). Labor shares in Iraq are from General Statistical Organization, Republic of Iraq, Annual Abstract of Statistics (Baghdad: Ministry of Planning), various issues. Estimates for Algeria, Egypt, Libya, and the Sudan are drawn from Economic Commission for Africa, Summaries of Economic Data (Addis Ababa, Ethiopia: ECA), various issues.

TABLE 7.4

Sectoral Product per Worker, Middle Eastern Countries, 1960s and 1970s[a]

Country	Early 1960s				Early 1970s			
	Agriculture[b]	Industry[c]	Services[d]	Industry and Services	Agriculture[b]	Industry[c]	Services[d]	Industry and Services
Major oil states								
Algeria	0.28	4.40	2.71	3.04	0.14	3.38	1.55	2.09
Iran	0.53	1.43	1.73	1.58	0.29	2.45	0.83	1.49
Iraq	0.35	4.73	0.78	1.63	0.32	4.60	1.06	1.86
Kuwait	0.40	2.13	0.42	1.01	0.15	2.14	0.42	1.02
Libya	0.27	1.95	1.20	1.43	0.10	3.09	0.60	1.39
Saudi Arabia	0.20	3.39	0.83	1.69	0.11	2.82	0.41	1.35
Other states								
Bahrain	—	—	—	—	0.14	2.21	0.41	1.06
Egypt	0.53	2.00	1.48	1.63	0.63	1.69	1.20	1.35
Israel	0.65	0.91	1.19	1.07	0.67	1.09	1.00	1.03
Jordan	0.46	0.54	1.79	1.29	0.48	—	—	1.21
Lebanon	0.44	—	—	1.21	0.47	0.88	1.23	1.12
Morocco	0.54	2.09	1.42	1.59	0.48	1.80	1.40	1.52
Southern Yemen	0.24	1.00	4.86	2.86	0.34	—	—	2.08
Sudan	0.67	2.50	3.38	3.00	0.43	5.00	5.88	5.64
Syria	0.53	1.24	1.50	1.42	0.31	1.28	2.14	1.80
Tunisia	0.36	1.39	3.85	2.42	0.36	1.42	1.92	1.72
Turkey	0.56	1.92	2.18	2.07	0.40	2.58	2.00	2.21

[a]Sectoral output per worker expressed as a ratio to countrywide product per worker.

[b]Includes farming, forestry, hunting, and fishing.

[c]Includes mining and quarrying, manufacturing, construction, and public utilities (electricity, gas, water, and sanitary services).

[d]Includes wholesale and retail trade, transport, storage, communications, finance, public administration, and personal services.

Sources: International Bank for Reconstruction and Development, World Tables (Washington, D.C.: IBRD), 1971 and 1975 issues; United Nations, Yearbook of National Accounts Statistics (New York: United Nations), various issues; International Labour Organization, Year Book of Labour Statistics, 1974 (Geneva: ILO, 1974); Central Planning Organization, Kingdom of Saudi Arabia, Development Plan 1390 A.H. (Riyadh: Government of Saudi Arabia, 1970); United States–Saudi Arabian Joint Commission on Economic Cooperation, Summary of Saudi Arabian Five Year Development Plan, 1975–1980 (Washington, D.C.: Department of the Treasury, 1975); General Statistical Organization, Republic of Iraq, Annual Abstract of Statistics (Baghdad: Ministry of Planning), various issues; and Economic Commission for Africa, Summaries of Economic Data (Addis Ababa, Ethiopia: ECA), various issues.

that sector's share in the labor force (74 in Table 7.3) gives 0.28. This means that the Algerian agriculture sector's per worker output was 28 percent of the nationwide product per worker. Everywhere in the Middle East, output per worker relative to the nationwide average is far lower in the agriculture sector than in the other sectors. For instance, in Libya in the early 1970s, the relative product of the industry sector was over 30 times as large as the relative agriculture sector product. On the other hand, the industry sector relative product in Israel was only 1.6 times that of the agriculture sector, indicating a wide range of relative productivities in the area. Generally, relative productivities in other sectors were at least two or three times that of the agriculture sector. These low agricultural relative productivities reflect the scarcity of complementary resources available to the agricultural labor in the area.

The ratio of the industry-plus-services sector to the agriculture sector measures intersectoral disparity in the relative labor productivities in a given country. The data show that disparity in sectoral productivities is tending to increase in the area. (See Table 7.5.) In the earlier period, ratios ranged from 1.65 to 11.92, with a geometric mean value of 4.13. In the later period, ratios for the same countries ranged from 1.54 to 14.96, with a geometric mean value of 5.30. In ten instances, disparity ratios increased; they decreased in only six. Disparity among the major oil states increased in every instance.

These disparities in relative sectoral products provide unweighted measures of inequality in sectoral output per worker. Utilizing Kuznets's method,[6] a weighted measure of inequality is the sum (signs disregarded) of the differences between sectoral shares in product and the labor force.* This measure of inequality can vary

---

*This measure is equivalent to the average of deviations of sectoral relatives of product per worker from 1 (signs disregarded), with the deviations being weighted by the shares of the sectors in the total labor force. Labor force shares are the appropriate weights for such output deviations. For an example of this equivalence, consider the data for Algeria in 1960 in Tables 7.1, 7.3, and 7.4. The Algerian agriculture sector's share in total product was 21.0 (Table 7.1), and its share in the labor force was 74 (Table 7.3). Subtracting the latter from the former yields -53.0. This value is equivalent to the difference between the agriculture sector's relative per worker share in production, 0.28 (Table 7.4), and the nationwide average product per worker (0.28 - 1.0 = -0.72), weighted by the agriculture sector's share in the labor force (-.72 × 74 = -53.28, rounded to -53.0). With this equivalence established, inequality in Algerian per worker sectoral products can be measured. In 1960, the differences in industry and

from zero to close to 200. The former represents the case of perfect equality, when the two series of shares are identical. The latter would occur in the extreme case of all the product being assigned to a single sector and that sector's share in the labor force being extremely small.

In the early 1970s, sectoral inequality was highest in the Sudan and Saudi Arabia; it was lowest in Israel. (See Table 7.5.) Inequality in sectoral-per-worker product was also especially high in Algeria and Libya. Change seems to have been substantial in Syria and the Sudan, where large increases in inequality occurred, and in Tunisia and Egypt, where substantial reductions took place.

In his study of 57 countries, Kuznets finds a strong negative long-term relationship between inequality and per capita income. Sectoral inequality declines significantly with a move from low to high per capita income.[7] In theory, factors of production would move toward higher marginal returns. If returns to labor are relatively low in agriculture, labor would tend to move from there into industry and services, lowering returns in the latter and raising marginal returns in agriculture. In the process, the total product of labor would tend to increase, per capita incomes would rise, and sectoral productivities would tend to equalize at the margin.

Assuming that ratios of averages at least approximately reflect marginal relationships, the industry plus services/agriculture ratios in Table 7.5 mean that in most countries the incentive to migrate from agriculture exists because of the relatively low average compensation there. But substantial reductions in sectoral inequalities may be a very long-term process, perhaps taking several generations to accomplish. Legal and political impediments may inhibit the movement of labor. Monopoly in industry and services would tend to lessen opportunities for employment there, thus maintaining disparities in compensation. Lack of information of opportunities elsewhere might retard the process of labor migration from agriculture. In the context of this process, the large increases in inequality in the Sudan and Syria seem especially perverse. The increases in agriculture's share in the labor force in these countries, with a widening disparity between agricultural and nonagricultural relative products and increasing inequality in sectoral products, do not imply improvement in the conditions of the agricultural populations in these countries. Only Israel with its low sectoral inequality and intersectoral disparity seems to meet these criteria of advanced economic development.

---

services sector shares in production and labor force were 17 and 36, respectively. The sum of the three sectoral differences, signs disregarded, is 106 (53 + 36 + 17).

TABLE 7.5

Intersectoral Disparity and Inequality in Sectoral Produce per Worker, Middle Eastern Countries, 1960s and 1970s

Country	Early 1960s		Early 1970s	
	Industry[a] + Services[b]/ Agriculture[c]	Inequality	Industry[a] + Services[b]/ Agriculture[c]	Inequality
Major oil states				
Algeria	10.86	106	14.96	96
Iran	2.98	52	5.14	70
Iraq	4.66	82	5.81	76
Kuwait	2.53	77	6.80	77
Libya	5.30	54	13.90	92
Saudi Arabia	8.45	86	12.27	102
Other states				
Bahrain	—	—	7.57	82
Egypt	3.08	54	2.14	36
Israel	1.65	18	1.54	6
Jordan	2.80	62	2.52	—
Lebanon	2.75	—	2.38	26
Morocco	2.94	52	3.17	52
Southern Yemen	11.92	108	6.12	—
Sudan	4.48	56	13.12	102
Syria	2.68	44	5.81	74
Tunisia	6.72	88	4.78	68
Turkey	3.70	62	5.53	80

[a]Industry sector includes mining and quarrying, manufacturing, construction, and public utilities (electricity, gas, water, and sanitary services).
[b]Services sector includes wholesale and retail trade, transport, storage, communications, finance, public administration, and personal services.
[c]Agriculture sector includes farming, forestry, hunting, and fishing.

Sources: International Bank for Reconstruction and Development, World Tables (Washington, D.C.: IBRD), 1971 and 1975 issues; United Nations, Yearbook of National Accounts Statistics (New York: United Nations), various issues; International Labour Organization, Year Book of Labour Statistics, 1974 (Geneva: ILO, 1974); Central Planning Organization, Kingdom of Saudi Arabia, Development Plan 1390 A.H. (Riyadh: Government of Saudi Arabia, 1970); United States–Saudi Arabian Joint Commission on Economic Cooperation, Summary of Saudi Arabian Five Year Development Plan, 1975–1980 (Washington, D.C.: Department of the Treasury, 1975); General Statistical Organization, Republic of Iraq, Annual Abstract of Statistics (Baghdad: Ministry of Planning), various issues; and Economic Commission for Africa, Summaries of Economic Data (Addis Ababa, Ethiopia: ECA), various issues.

The oil states would seem to be exceptions to Kuznets's findings, and inequality in their sectoral returns per worker serves to highlight the lopsidedness of their economic structures. Inequality is higher in these countries than in such lower-income countries as Egypt, Morocco, and Tunisia. The relatively high degree of inequality in sectoral returns in the petroleum-exporting countries reflects the tenuous relation between high oil incomes and general economic development.

In pointing to these conclusions, it should be emphasized that the time series used are both short and subject to a considerable degree of error. Even so, the findings confirm in a general way that structural imbalance is still the predominant industrial characteristic of the Middle East.

STRUCTURE OF COMMODITY TRADE

The postwar oil boom has exerted an uneven influence on the Middle East as an international trading community. At the present time, the economies of the petroleum exporters are the most open, that is, the ones most exposed to external economic forces. Among them, trade as a fraction of GNP (an index of openness) ranged from 30 to 80 percent in 1974, but among the other states, trade ranged from only 10 to 35 percent. (See Table 7.6.) Little or no increase in openness has occurred among the states without large oil reserve holdings in the past decade or so. In contrast, the growth of the world's demand for oil and the rise in oil's share in world trade have served to draw the petroleum exporters more deeply into the international exchange system and to increase their openness. States with large oil reserve holdings are the ones most sensitive to world inflation and recession, as well as such random shocks as crop failure and changes in trade policy elsewhere in the international community.

Significant changes in the composition of trade have occurred in several countries. As it became more industrialized, Israel, for example, succeeded in increasing the share of manufactured goods in total exports to about 75 percent, from less than 60 percent in the mid-1950s. At the same time, food and consumer goods' share of imports declined, while the share of intermediate goods and capital equipment increased. In Morocco, Syria, and Tunisia, the share of machinery in total imports has risen substantially, while the share of manufactures in exports has risen.

Deliberate change in the structure of trade represents a strategy of development available to the economies of the developing countries. Initial industrial development that permits the substitution of domestically produced goods for those that formerly had to be imported

TABLE 7.6

Economic Openness and the Direction of Trade, Middle Eastern Countries, 1963 and 1974
(percent)

Country	Openness[a]	Shares in Middle Eastern Trade					
		Exports			Imports		
		Developed Market Economies	Communist States	Third World	Developed Market Economies	Communist States	Third World
Major oil states							
Algeria							
1963	.34	96.5	0.0	3.5	94.3	0.0	5.7
1974	.33	88.3	6.4	5.3	90.5	4.3	5.2
Iran							
1963	.16	70.3	3.5	26.2	79.1	11.3	9.6
1974	.33	88.1	0.0	11.9	86.1	5.6	8.3
Iraq							
1963	.31	87.5	1.6	10.9	59.8	20.0	20.2
1974	.39	75.5	0.8	23.7	73.0	10.6	16.4
Kuwait							
1963	.43	93.6	0.0	6.4	74.8	0.9	24.3
1974	.61	69.1	0.6	30.3	74.7	5.3	20.0
Libya							
1963	.51	97.9	0.1	2.0	89.2	5.1	5.7
1974	.47	85.1	2.4	12.5	86.3	4.2	9.5
Oman							
1963	.29[b]	33.3	0.0	66.7	76.5	6.0	23.5
1974	.74	93.8	0.0	6.2	78.8	0.0	21.2
Qatar							
1963	—	95.8	0.0	4.2	73.0	0.0	27.0
1974	.83	54.1	0.0	45.9	68.0	2.6	29.4

Saudi Arabia							
1963	.37	79.7	0.0	20.3	77.0	0.0	23.0
1974	.75	78.8	0.0	21.2	75.3	1.6	23.1
United Arab Emirates							
1963c	—	88.0	0.0	12.0	98.9	0.0	1.1
1974	.67	96.8	0.0	3.2	67.1	0.0	32.9
Other states							
Bahrain							
1963	—	83.2	0.0	16.8	84.7	0.0	15.3
1974	.54	76.6	0.0	23.4	71.1	7.0	21.9
Egypt							
1963	.22	36.0	44.8	19.2	67.6	18.0	14.4
1974	.19	45.6	40.8	13.6	80.0	7.4	12.6
Israel							
1963	.33	83.1	2.7	14.2	84.6	2.0	13.4
1974	.32	76.6	0.6	22.8	61.7	0.2	38.1
Jordan							
1963	.32	11.8	7.8	80.4	58.8	9.9	31.3
1974	.29	13.4	1.7	84.9	53.5	7.0	39.5
Lebanon							
1963	.41	30.0	9.3	60.7	65.1	8.4	26.5
1974	.35d	47.9	4.5	47.6	79.1	5.3	15.6
Morocco							
1963	.22	81.3	10.6	8.1	78.5	13.4	8.1
1974	.26	78.1	10.9	11.0	74.5	7.0	18.5
Northern Yemen							
1963	—	50.0	0.0	50.0	9.1	0.0	90.9
1974	.09	66.7	14.1	19.2	55.1	7.8	37.1
Southern Yemen							
1963	—	33.9	0.0	66.1	36.2	2.5	61.3
1974	.11	75.4	2.1	22.5	35.7	6.4	57.9

(continued)

TABLE 7.6 (continued)

Country	Openness[a]	Exports			Imports		
		Developed Market Economies	Communist States	Third World	Developed Market Economies	Communist States	Third World
Sudan							
1963	.21	60.9	19.1	20.0	65.0	12.5	22.5
1974	.15	56.6	22.6	20.8	70.7	14.5	14.8
Syria							
1963	.25	36.8	32.6	30.6	65.8	11.2	23.0
1974	.25	55.6	26.0	18.4	65.1	15.8	19.1
Tunisia							
1963	.22	81.3	6.1	12.6	86.2	6.1	7.7
1974	.29	75.1	5.6	19.3	80.1	3.7	16.2
Turkey							
1963	.08	81.6	9.7	8.7	81.9	7.3	10.8
1974	.09	72.8	10.2	17.0	73.8	5.0	21.2

[a] A country's openness to foreign trade is the ratio of its average trade to its GNP:

$$\frac{\text{Exports} + \text{Imports}}{2} \div \text{GNP}$$

[b] Refers to 1967.
[c] Refers to the Trucial States.
[d] Refers to 1973.

Note: Developed market economies include the non-Communist European countries, North America, Japan, Australia, New Zealand, and South Africa. The Communist states are those of Eastern Europe, as well as the USSR, the People's Republic of China, North Korea, North Vietnam, and Cuba. All others are treated as being part of the Third World.

Sources: International Monetary Fund, Direction of Trade (Washington, D.C.: IMF), various issues. GNP estimates used are from International Bank for Reconstruction and Development, World Tables (Washington, D.C.: IBRD), 1971 and 1975 issues; and United Nations, Yearbook of National Accounts Statistics (New York: United Nations), various issues.

saves foreign exchange, and these savings can be used to import the capital goods needed for further industrialization. If new investment leads to increased output that can find a place in world markets, the increased export earnings can be used for additional equipment and so forth. Thus, growth can be induced by the interplay of export expansion and import substitution in those economies having the necessary labor skills.

In a few instances, important shifts in the direction of trade have occurred, as, for example, the greatly increased importance of Egypt's imports from the West, but in most cases, change has been slight. The exports of the area are still largely agricultural and mineral primary products, while its import needs are mainly the industrial products of the more developed nations. Thus, the West and Japan are the area's natural trading partners, although the USSR and the more developed states of the Communist bloc represent alternative sources of industrial products and outlets for raw materials. Since states attempt to influence the policies of one another, partly through commercial ties, the area's continued involvement with the West carries geopolitical as well as economic implications.

POPULATION GROWTH AND AGE STRUCTURE

In recent years, the spread of Western science to the Third World has produced a precipitous decline in death rates. Knowledge resulting from 200 years' accumulation in the West can produce stunning results almost simultaneously with application. In one instructive example, death rates fell in Sri Lanka from 20 per 1,000 persons to 14 per 1,000 in one year, 1946-47, after spraying with DDT destroyed the malarial mosquito there.[8] Through control of disease, death rates have declined in the Middle East, as elsewhere, but birth rates have remained high or have even risen in several cases. The general result has been accelerated population growth.

In the Middle East, birthrates range from 30 to 50 per 1,000, while death rates are 10 to 20 per 1,000. Together, these rates determine the rate of natural increase (see Table 7.7), and with migration, they produce the actual rate of population growth. In recent years, net immigration has been an important contributor to actual population growth in Israel, Kuwait, and the Arab states of the Gulf.* Although

---

*Although manpower flows are difficult to measure, as many enter illegally and are unrecorded, they are of substantial magnitude and will have a definite impact on the growth and structure of the populations of the area.

TABLE 7.7

Components of Natural Population Growth, Middle Eastern Countries,
Mid-1970s

Country	Crude Birth- Rate	Crude Death Rate	Rate of Natural Increase
Major oil states			
Algeria	48.7	15.4	3.3
Iran	45.3	15.6	3.0
Iraq	48.1	14.6	3.4
Kuwait	47.1	5.3	4.2
Libya	45.0	14.7	3.0
Saudi Arabia	49.5	20.2	2.9
Other states			
Egypt	35.5	12.4	2.3
Israel	28.3	7.2	2.1
Jordan	47.6	14.7	3.3
Lebanon	39.8	9.9	3.0
Morocco	46.2	15.7	3.1
Northern Yemen	49.6	20.6	2.9
Southern Yemen	49.6	20.6	2.9
Sudan	47.8	17.5	3.0
Syria	45.4	15.4	3.0
Tunisia	40.0	13.8	2.6
Turkey	39.6	12.5	2.7

Note: Birth- and death rates are expressed in terms of per
1,000 persons per annum.

Source: United Nations, Demographic Yearbook, 1975 (New
York: United Nations, 1976).

some impressive reductions in the birthrate have occurred in recent
years, notably in Iran, Egypt, and Tunisia, birthrates in most of the
states remain among the highest in the world.

As in the Third World at large, the difficulty in improving welfare through increasing per capita output in the Middle East is compounded by rapid population growth. Incremental product tends to be
absorbed by new population without significant per capita betterment.
Birthrates are culturally determined and are not readily changed by
public policy. Rates will fall in the Middle East when additional chil-

TABLE 7.8

Age Structure of the Population, Middle Eastern Countries, 1960 and 1970

| | Percentages of Population | | | | Dependency Ratio | |
| | 1960 | | 1970 | | | |
Country	0-14	65+	0-14	65+	1960	1970
Major oil states						
Algeria	44.0	4.0	47.0	5.0	92.3	108.3
Iran	42.0	4.0	47.0	3.0	85.2	100.0
Iraq	45.0	5.0	48.0	4.0	100.0	108.3
Kuwait	38.0	2.0	43.0	2.0	66.7	81.8
Libya	43.0	5.0	44.0	5.0	92.3	96.1
Oman	—	—	45.0	3.0	—	92.3
Qatar	—	—	—	—	—	—
Saudi Arabia	—	—	44.2	2.7	—	88.3
United Arab Emirates	—	—	34.0	3.0	—	58.7
Other states						
Bahrain	—	—	44.0	3.0	—	88.7
Egypt	43.0	3.0	44.0	4.0	85.2	92.3
Israel	36.1	5.2	33.3	6.5	70.4	66.1
Jordan	45.0	4.0	47.0	3.0	96.1	100.0
Lebanon	44.0	4.0	43.0	5.0	92.3	92.3
Morocco	44.0	4.0	46.0	5.0	92.3	104.1
Northern Yemen	—	—	40.0	5.0	—	81.8
Southern Yemen	47.0	2.0	45.0	3.0	96.1	92.3
Sudan	46.0	5.0	46.0	4.0	104.1	100.0
Syria	42.0	5.0	45.0	4.0	88.7	96.1
Tunisia	42.0	5.0	45.0	4.0	88.7	96.1
Turkey	41.3	3.5	41.8	4.3	81.2	85.5

Note: The dependency ratio is the population of less than 15 and more than 64 years of age divided by the population 15 through 64 years times 100.

Source: International Bank for Reconstruction and Development, World Tables, 1975 (Washington, D.C.: IBRD, 1976).

dren are seen as alternatives to a higher standard of living rather than as status symbols, old-age insurance, or cheap labor. Until that time, the economic consequences of rapid population growth will have to be endured.

An increase in the rate of population growth stimulates present consumption at the expense of capital formation. A growing population leads to increasing pressure on existing herds, housing, and available supplies of water and arable land. An expanding and more youthful population also means more pressure on the state to increase the supply of services associated with child rearing, such as education and pediatric medicine. Consequently, the resources needed for capital formation tend to be harder to accumulate, as the population becomes larger, more youthful, and more dependent.

In the long run, the age structure will reflect the faster population growth, and the labor force will tend to grow at a rate equal to the growth rate of the population. The faster growth of the labor force means that favorable factor proportions will be harder to maintain. If growth in the labor force outruns the growth of capital and other resources, the marginal productivity of labor will fall, as will per capita income. Thus, rapid population growth tends to stimulate the desire to consume, but it tends also to impair the capacity of the economy to increase per capita output. This conflict between desire and capability is one of the sources of tension that is typically part of the development process in the Third World and one that can lead to social unrest and violent political change.

As populations of Middle Eastern countries have become more youthful, dependency ratios have risen and are now high in relation to the 50-to-60 range found among the more developed countries. (See Table 7.8.) This trend implies a growing burden of responsibility for working-age populations and increasing savings difficulties in the states without large petroleum resources. The long-term difficulty faced by rapidly growing, youthful populations becomes all the more apparent when it is recognized that human resource development is an integral part of the economic growth process. Capital formation implies investment in human as well as nonhuman resources.

EDUCATION AND HUMAN RESOURCES

Modern economic growth theorists only recently have begun to pay attention to the role of investment in human beings. This lack of interest may have been in part the result of the Keynesian revolution, with its emphasis on the relation between intended real savings and business investment in enterprise. The emphasis of the influential Harrod-Domar model on physical capital and its relation to output probably served to divert attention from human resources. Soviet development strategy, with its emphasis on the accumulation of heavy industrial capital, has undoubtedly also had great influence on Third World planners. Whatever its causes, the neglect of the study of human wealth ended in the 1960s, with new emphasis in the works of Theodore W. Schultz and others.[9] Research supports the conclusion that returns on investment in human resources through health and education services are relatively high.

There can be little doubt that basic literacy is a necessary quality for a productive labor force, and investment in this goal surely promises high returns in the Middle East. Higher levels of skills are required if innovative management and technical resources are to be developed. A deficiency in human capital limits the capability of an economy to absorb nonhuman capital and other cooperant resources, and with the increasing value of petroleum resources, it is probable that a shortage of human capital represents a greater obstacle to regional development than do physical nonhuman capital limitations.

In most Middle Eastern countries, less than 50 percent of the adult population is literate. (See Table 1.2.) Although estimates of labor force literacy are not available, literacy among males of 15 years or more provides a serviceable approximation, as the very limited extent of female participation in economic activity means that the labor forces of the area are almost entirely male. For the Arab countries as a group, about 60 percent of males over 15 years old were illiterate in 1970. This can be put in context by noting that in industrial countries adult males are more than 90 percent literate.

Acute shortages of modern skills is the inevitable concomitant of the low literacy levels found in the Middle East. Members of the professional and skilled technical classes represent small fractions of the labor force. Doctors are few in relation to the population, as are teachers at the higher levels of education. Executive and managerial personnel are in particularly short supply. The consistent exception to these observations is Israel, which is well supplied with modern skills and thus serves as a reference point for gauging the deficiencies elsewhere. (See Table 7.9.)

These widespread manpower shortages represent an intractable development problem for the area as a whole. The affluent oil states can draw skills from the rest of the area, but this tends to be expensive for both sending and receiving countries. While the manpower-supplying states gain such obvious benefits as the stream of foreign exchange remittances sent home by overseas nationals and reduced domestic unemployment, they also incur the costs implied by the loss of skills needed for their own development. The labor-importing oil states are in need of high- and middle-level skills, so that their development efforts will attract some of the best brains in the region.

TABLE 7.9

Skilled Manpower, Middle Eastern Countries, Early 1970s

Country	High-Level Manpower as Percentage of the Labor Force		Medical and Educational Skills per 10,000 Population		
	Professionals and Technicians	Administrators, Executives, and Managers	Doctors	Second-Level Teachers	Third-Level Teachers
Major oil states					
Algeria	3.4[a]	0.8[a]	1.3	9.7	1.3
Iran	2.7[a]	0.1[a]	3.2	18.4	3.2
Iraq	—	—	4.0	15.4	2.5
Kuwait	10.7	0.7	12.5	77.5	3.5
Libya	3.1[a]	1.4[a]	7.9	30.6	2.8
Qatar	—	—	5.8	30.5	—
Saudi Arabia	4.8[a]	0.5[b]	3.8	17.4	2.2
United Arab Emirates	—	—	6.6	29.0	—
Other states					
Bahrain	8.0	1.7	5.7	—	1.7
Egypt	4.4[a]	1.6[a]	6.6	17.8	4.7
Israel	16.5	3.2	27.4	44.3	20.5
Jordan	4.0[b]	0.5[b]	4.2	21.6	1.6
Lebanon	9.2	1.9	7.7	22.7[a]	9.8
Morocco	4.0	1.0	0.8	10.3	0.4
Northern Yemen	—	—	0.4	—	0.1
Southern Yemen	—	—	0.4	7.5	0.3
Sudan	2.5	0.3	0.4	2.7	0.4
Syria	4.3	0.2	2.8	31.3	1.8
Tunisia	4.0[a]	0.7[a]	1.9	13.1	1.2
Turkey	3.2	0.4	4.7	14.5	3.1

[a]Refers to the mid-1960s.
[b]Author's estimate.

Sources: International Labour Office, Year Book of Labour Statistics (Geneva: ILO), various issues; United Nations, Statistical Yearbook (New York: United Nations), various issues; and United Nations Educational, Scientific, and Cultural Organization, Statistical Yearbook (Paris: UNESCO), various issues.

For their part, the labor-receiving countries benefit from the availability of skills that otherwise would be missing, but there are also substantial costs that have to be weighed against their productivity in determining the added social value of the immigrants.

International competition for foreign labor requires that the importing countries not only pay attractive wages but also provide housing facilities and such extra amenities as medical services and non-traditional imported goods. Thus, the importation of relatively large supplies of foreign labor may imply substantial extra infrastructure costs. Unless certain minimum prerequisites are provided, work stoppages and labor unrest will impose social costs of other kinds. In addition, if the families of the immigrants are allowed to join them, extra medical and educational costs will have to be added. In the later 1970s, both labor-supplying and -receiving nations were increasingly concerned about the costs implied by the continuing flow of manpower into the affluent oil states.

Among the expanding oil economies of the Gulf, a new ethnic division of labor is emerging. In the past, manpower imported by the Arab countries was composed largely of manual labor from Oman or the Yemen, with some admixture of administrative personnel from India, Iran, or historic Palestine. Today, a much greater diversity in skills and resources is apparent. Western Europe and the United States are leading suppliers of high-level technical and professional manpower, while Lebanon, Egypt, India, and Pakistan provide middle-level technicians, administrators, and clerks. Jordan and Egypt continue to be prime sources of teachers, as, to a lesser extent, is the Sudan. South Korea and Pakistan are major suppliers of skilled and semiskilled manual labor in the construction and service industries. By 1975, nonnationals made up 35 percent of the combined population of the Arab Gulf states and 60 percent of the combined labor force.* Dependence on foreign workers to such an extent can lead to serious social problems. Nationals may feel politically and culturally threatened, while guest workers may be dissatisfied with their housing and working conditions and with what they perceive as their lack of opportunity for political and cultural expression.

Among the manpower-supplying Middle Eastern countries, productivity losses are most serious in Jordan, Lebanon, and the Sudan. Transfers of teachers, skilled manual workers, and technicians from these countries have reached the point at which long-term domestic growth is being jeopardized. Even in Egypt, the archetypal labor sur-

---

*The states referred to are Bahrain, Kuwait, Qatar, Saudi Arabia, and the United Arab Emirates.

plus economy, shortages in the ranks of skilled machine operators and construction workers were beginning to appear in the later 1970s.[10]

Thus, when manpower transfers are considered from the standpoint of regional costs and benefits, the process appears to be reaching its efficient limits sooner than might have been expected. The ultimate resolution of the Middle East's skill shortages depends on coordinated manpower development within the region; but when adult literacy rates are low, it may be many years before substantial numbers of suitably prepared young people are available for professional specialization.

At the present time, the Middle Eastern Countries are engaged in a bootstrap effort to ease their manpower problems by ensuring basic literacy at the lower end of the population age structure. In the 1960s, primary school enrollments increased sharply and continued to grow in the 1970s. Beginning at a low base, enrollment growth was especially rapid in the states of the Arabian peninsula. Even so, most countries have not yet achieved full enrollment at the primary level, and the ratios of enrolled students to student-age populations in most instances are unsatisfactorily low at the secondary level. (See Table 7.10.) The difficulties involved in a regional educational effort are suggested by the generally high ratios of pupils to teachers at the primary level. Through the constraint it imposes on instruction, manpower shortage tends to be self-perpetuating. Rapid population growth compounds the problem. In general, an indigenous solution to the Middle East's manpower problem still seems remote.

Relative emphasis on manpower development can be assessed in terms of public expenditure on education as a fraction of GNP. (See Table 7.11.) Among the main geographic areas of the Middle East, the shares of resources allotted to education are particularly large in the Maghreb. However, the financial strength of the oil states is reflected in their higher absolute outlays per pupil. Average expenditures per enrolled student are many times greater in the Gulf region than in the nonoil countries. But these financial differences do not accurately measure variations in the quality of instruction. Education is more costly per unit among the newly rich states of the Gulf. As their populations are small and their programs are of recent origin, the possibilities of scale economies are severely circumscribed, and they have been forced to purchase educational resources abroad at a time of worldwide inflation. This pertains especially to human resources. Teachers' salaries are the predominant element in recurring educational cost, and premium wages have to be paid to attract and hold teachers from elsewhere in the Middle East and beyond. These factors combine to make the unit costs of a given standard of education substantially higher in the Gulf.

TABLE 7.10

School Enrollment and Pupil/Teacher Ratios, Middle Eastern Countries, 1970s

| Country | Gross School Enrollment Ratios | | | | | | Pupil/Teacher Ratios (circa 1973) | | |
| | Level 1 | | Level 2 | | Level 3 | | Level 1 | Level 2 | Level 3 |
	1970	1975	1970	1975	1970	1975			
Major oil states									
Algeria	75	88	12	21	1	2	43	27	10
Iran	79*		37*		4*		30	30	12
Iraq	69	93	—	—	—	7	24	25	23
Kuwait	62	61	89	84	4	6	18	12	23
Libya	111	144	21	50	3	6	24	13	13
Oman	3	52	—	1	2	—	30	9	—
Qatar	115	157	38	82	—	5	20	12	14
Saudi Arabia	34	47	9	19	1	2	21	14	10
United Arab Emirates	73	117	11	40	—	—	26	20	—
Other states									
Bahrain	109	103	47	51	1	3	21	—	—
Egypt	71	72	34	41	6	11	41	27	19
Israel	136*		34*		22*		14	9	8
Jordan	73	84	33	44	2	4	37	21	17
Lebanon	103	114	50	55	18	19	14	—	16
Morocco	43	50	15	18	1	2	40	21	15
Northern Yemen	10	23	1	3	—	1	38	—	—
Southern Yemen	59	80	9	23	—	1	29	19	—
Sudan	32	38	6	12	1	1	39	24	15
Syria	89	103	39	49	6	9	36	19	—
Tunisia	100	95	26	23	2	3	41	21	10
Turkey	105*		32*		5*		32	27	16

*School enrollment ratios refer to 1972.

Note: Levels 1, 2, and 3 refer to ages 6 through 11, 12 through 17, and 18 through 23, respectively. School enrollment ratios can exceed 100 when the actual enrolled age distribution exceeds the official school-age definition.

Sources: United Nations, Statistical Yearbook (New York: United Nations), various issues; United Nations Educational, Scientific and Cultural Organization, Statistical Yearbook (Paris: UNESCO), various issues; and idem, "Recent Quantitative Trends and Projections Concerning Enrollment in Education in the Arab Countries" (Mimeographed paper prepared by the UNESCO Division of Statistics on Education, Paris, for the Conference of Ministers of Education and those responsible for economic planning in the Arab states, United Arab Emirates, November 7-16, 1977).

TABLE 7.11

Educational Emphasis and Cost, Middle Eastern Countries,
1963, 1973, and 1974

Country	Public Expenditures on Education as Percentage of Current GNP			Educational Outlays per Pupil—1974 (current U.S. dollars)
	1963	1973	1974	
Major oil states				
Algeria	3.1	8.3	6.5	250
Iran	3.2	3.7	3.3	235
Iraq	6.6	4.4	3.6	154
Kuwait	2.5	2.9	2.6	1,412
Libya	4.1	6.8	4.0	654
Oman	—	—	2.1	451
Qatar	—	—	4.7	917
Saudi Arabia	7.7	5.4	4.6	1,264
United Arab Emirates	—	—	1.7	1,641
Other states				
Bahrain	—	6.3	3.1	322
Egypt	5.8	4.3	5.5	85
Israel	5.7	3.6	3.4	435
Jordan	3.1	2.5	3.9	87
Lebanon	2.1	2.6	3.0	114
Morocco	3.9	5.7	5.3	163
Northern Yemen	0.1	1.2	0.6	23
Southern Yemen	—	6.3	4.0	53
Sudan	2.0	4.5	8.0	139
Syria	5.0	3.8	3.7	116
Tunisia	5.8	6.0	7.0	186
Turkey	3.5	2.9	2.7	112

Sources: United Nations Educational, Scientific and Cultural Organization, Statistical Yearbook, 1975 (Paris: UNESCO, 1976); Ruth L. Sivard, World Military and Social Expenditures, 1976 (Leesburg, Va.: World Military and Social Publications, 1976); and United Nations Educational, Scientific and Cultural Organization, "Recent Quantitative Trends and Projections Concerning Enrollment in Education in the Arab Countries" (Mimeographed paper prepared by the UNESCO Division of Statistics on Education, Paris, for the Conference of Ministers of Education and those responsible for Economic Planning in the Arab States, United Arab Emirates, November 7-16, 1977).

There is a circular relationship between underdevelopment and skill shortage. Underdevelopment constrains manpower training, while skilled manpower shortages tend to sustain underdevelopment. Shortages are most acute among middle-level administrators and professionals, but a surplus of manpower often exists among low-skilled clerical and office workers and among university-trained personnel, whose skills are not needed by the existing economy. The underlying problem is that curricula have not been adequately adjusted to the needs of development, and, in addition, incentive systems do not adequately guide labor into the socially more valuable occupations. In some cases, regulations prevent relative wages from accurately reflecting relative productivities. A persistent problem is the traditional low regard for manual labor and industrial occupations, as greater status and prestige are associated more closely with white-collar clerical jobs in the state bureaucracy than with the blue-collar occupations, even though the latter often are of higher social value.

Although productive but low-status occupations can be made more attractive by wage adjustments, fundamental changes in social values occur only in the long run and may defy official manipulation altogether. The alteration of curricula may be difficult because effective change in this direction is impossible without competent teaching personnel in expanded programs. Higher education abroad offers means to more rapidly increasing skills, but this is costly and may, in the end, only contribute to the flow of trained manpower to higher wage areas. In the final analysis, an adequate response to the problem of skilled manpower shortage will be possible only when larger volumes of persons pass through the first and second levels of education and become available for industrial and advanced academic training.

ENTREPRENEURSHIP AND INNOVATION

Risk bearing and innovation are the essential qualities of entrepreneurship, making it the factor of production that generates much of the dynamic of economic development. It is a necessary ingredient of sustained, long-term growth, irrespective of the distributions of property rights or decision-making responsibilities. Successful enterprise, public as well as private, needs this element.

It is impossible to measure the supply of entrepreneurs in most of the countries of the area, but certain factors may be cited that attest to their relative scarcity. For one thing, it is reasonable to assume a positive correlation between education and entrepreneurial ability. High-level manpower scarcity implies a scarcity of innovative talent. A thorough study of management in Lebanon by Yusif

Sayigh supports the assumption that successful entrepreneurship is positively correlated with level of education. [11]

In a survey of some 8,000 Lebanese establishments, Sayigh identified 207 innovators, for a rate of entrepreneurial occurrence of only 2.6 percent. Of the 207, 58 percent had finished high school and 35 percent had finished college. These rates of higher education were far more than those of the general population of Lebanon. Only about 2 percent were without any formal education. The scarcity of entrepreneurship in the Middle East at large may be inferred from this survey, as the Lebanese economy is widely recognized as having a relatively large supply of talented businessmen and educated persons. Now, after centuries of stagnation and foreign domination, the new Middle Eastern oil revenues can provide a catalyst for a resurgence of the entrepreneurial spirit.

The economic development of Europe and the United States in the nineteenth century was enhanced by technological innovation, in which entrepreneurs found ways of incorporating hitherto untried inventions into the production process. Today, world technology represents a huge storehouse of methods and techniques waiting to be employed in developing areas. Thus, in the Third World, the innovation needed is more adaptive than originative in character. The needed entrepreneurial function is one of combining elements of advanced technology, selected from abroad, with available domestic factors in the production process.

An essential part of efficient technological borrowing is on-site research, as products and methods from abroad usually need to be adapted to local conditions. In the Middle East, and in the Third World generally, the innovating spirit can be fostered by building local institutions and directing personnel training toward solving domestic production problems, reducing bottlenecks, and the like. Adaptive innovation of this sort explains much of Israel's success in many fields of enterprise. [12] Other hopeful signs are appearing elsewhere. For instance, Jordan's Royal Scientific Society aspires to become a vehicle for transferring Western technology to the Arab world. In the mid-1970s, it initiated a program for adapting international solar energy technology to Middle Eastern conditions and undertook experimentation with a solar-powered desalination plant at Aqaba. In addition, a promising expansion of programs was undertaken by the Kuwait Institute for Scientific Research. Finally, a cardinal principle of policy among the major oil-exporting countries is that oil should be traded not just for cash but for specific elements of Western technology as well.

These promising signs notwithstanding, only small fractions of available supplies of scientists, engineers, and technicians in the Middle East have been employed in R&D. (See Table 7.12.) Due to the

TABLE 7.12

Indicators of Scientific Capability and R&D Effort, Middle Eastern Countries, Early 1970s

Country	Scientific Manpower per 10,000 Population			
	Scientists and Engineers		Technicians	
	Total	In R&D	Total	In R&D
Major oil states				
Algeria	—	0.2	—	0.1
Iran	41.8	1.6	10.7	0.3
Iraq	8.1	0.1	15.1	0.0
Kuwait	54.9	—	73.5	—
Other states				
Egypt	—	2.1	—	—
Israel	124.6	10.7	138.4	—
Jordan	—	0.2	—	0.3
Lebanon	21.4	1.0	—	—
Sudan	8.6	0.2	1.6	0.1
Turkey	—	1.8	—	—

Country	Expenditures on R&D (U.S. dollars)		
	Percent GNP	Per Capita	Per Scientist and Engineer
Major oil states			
Algeria	0.3	1.12	70,742
Iran	0.5	2.13	12,986
Iraq	0.1	0.17	13,260
Other states			
Israel	1.4	31.93	31,720
Turkey	0.3	1.21	—

Source: United Nations Educational, Scientific, and Cultural Organization, Statistical Yearbook (Paris: UNESCO), issues 1970-75.

fact that, in most cases, programs are too small to permit a lowering of support costs per scientist through economies of scale, rates
of R&D expenditures per scientist are fairly high in relation to world
standards. Thus, it seems clear that a regional approach, involving
the pooling of resources to solve common problems, should serve to
lower unit costs and to obtain better returns from outlays.

In some cases, institutional features and incentive systems in
the area impede entrepreneurial activity. This appears to be true
particularly in the socialist economies. In a recent study of Egyptian
management, Saleh Farid points to several causes of declining entrepreneurship.[13] Farid's work shows that education alone is not enough
to provide for the adaptive innovations needed for modern development. Of 96 directors of state enterprises studied, 67 percent were
college graduates, and nearly 89 percent had at least finished high
school. Although all of the directors had prior business experience,
they shared an unwillingness to take risks and a preference for the
status quo. A look at Egyptian industrial organization provides an
explanation.

In Nasser's day, directors of state enterprises in Egypt were
supervised by the minister of the sector in question and, more directly, by one of several corporations. Egyptian public sector corporations resembled U.S. holding companies in their relation to production units. In the abstract, this appeared to be a reasonable control structure, but, in practice, several difficulties arose. For one
thing, appointments to the boards of state enterprises tended to be
political in nature. More experienced persons sometimes were rejected for service on boards in favor of less qualified but politically
more trustworthy candidates. While salaries were not high enough
to attract the more successful entrepreneurs, they were sufficient to
attract military officers and veteran civil servants. Subsequently,
many experienced entrepreneurs emigrated to establish new careers
and businesses in Lebanon, Canada, and elsewhere.

In Egypt, lines of responsibility between corporations and state
enterprises were not clear; consequently, board members hesitated
to initiate long-term policy. Occasional intervention in management
by the corporations tended to weaken board morale. At the same
time, the centralization of decision making, the concentration of the
means of production in the hands of the state, the extension of central
planning, and price control meant that emphasis was on production
and not on the introduction of new methods or new products. Furthermore, centralization meant that the role of consumer demand in guiding the pattern of production was reduced, that domestic competition
was suppressed, and that state firms were shielded from foreign competition by import controls. The result was the absence of sufficient
incentive to innovate. Further consequences were lags between plan-

ning and implementation, failure to take local conditions into account, and delays in payments to suppliers for inputs and deliveries of products to buyers. These problems are likely to be shared by other states in which economic decision making has become highly centralized. When enterprise is the captive of state bureaucracy, dynamism tends to be lost.

With "denasserization," the managements of production units have been given more operational autonomy, including the right to raise capital. While such liberalization is a positive step, the reforms probably have not gone far enough. The most commonly heard explanation of the failure of foreign capital to move into Egypt in the mid-1970s was the continuing disincentive to creative action provided by excessive red tape and bureaucratic control.

URBANIZATION

Because rising shares of the industrial and services sector in output and the labor force imply the increasing concentration of economic resources, structural change has a spatial dimension. This process of spatial concentration is implied by the term underlined urbanization.

There are net economies of scale to be expected from urbanization, but there is inevitably some optimal size for all cities, after which diseconomies will offset the economies. As urban pressure rises, asset prices, land values, and rents also rise. Congestion costs mount, as more time is spent in queuing. Labor costs rise for firms. As public utilities pass their optimal scales of plant, costs per unit of output increase. Urban life loses its attractiveness, as public services degenerate, the cost of living rises, and the frictions derived from congestion increase. These factors imply that as urban density per square mile grows, urban net economies will rise, reach some maximum level, and then decline. While it is true that technological progress in the production of urban services can postpone the onset of decline, it seems likely that this point has already been reached and passed in many cities of the Third World. When rapid population growth, low agricultural labor productivity, and municipal welfare services combine, the effect is the collection of masses of unskilled labor in urban settings at rates too fast to permit their absorption into productive employment through formal skill creation or on-the-job training. When this happens, urban services may be overwhelmed, and there is the danger that degeneration will set in without potential productivity gains having been realized. The crush of slums around most Third World cities is evidence of the problem.

Urbanization is an ongoing process in the world at large; between 1950 and 1970, the urban share of world population rose from

TABLE 7.13

Urbanization in the Middle East
(percent)

Country	Annual Rate of Population Growth—1967-74		Urban Percentage of the Total Population		
	Urban	Rural	1960	1967	1974
Major oil states					
Algeria	6.8	0.2	31	41	52
Iran	4.6	1.8	33	39	43
Iraq	6.3	0.3	40	54	64
Libya	5.6	3.0	23	26	30
Other states					
Bahrain	3.8	1.6	75	78	81
Egypt	3.3	1.7	38	41	44
Israel	4.0	0.5	76	78	82
Jordan	4.0	3.4	40	41	42
Lebanon	6.0	-0.6	31	49	60
Morocco	5.6	2.6	29	33	38
Southern Yemen	6.4	1.7	22	27	33
Sudan	5.5	2.2	9	11	13
Syria	4.7	2.2	37	42	46
Turkey	4.9	0.7	32	36	43

Sources: United Nations, Monthly Bulletin of Statistics 25, no. 11, "Special Table B" (New York: United Nations, 1971); idem, Statistical Yearbook, 1975 (New York: United Nations, 1976); idem, Demographic Yearbook, 1975 (New York: United Nations, 1976).

28 to 37 percent.[14] As industry or services replaces agriculture as the prime source of income, urbanization will create profound changes in the patterns of life and work of a population. Skills and values needed for successful urban development are different from those required for a rural, subsistence economy, and interdependence is far greater among members of an urban society. Urbanization holds the promise of increased individual prosperity through specialization and increasing productivity, but when the disparate parts of an urban system fail to develop evenly, retrogression and despair can replace hope and progress, leading to political instability and repression.

Comparisons of urban size are not always reliable because numerical definitions of urban population vary internationally. In view of this difficulty, discussion here is limited to changes within nations through time.

Estimates indicate that the extent of urbanization increased in every country of the area during the past decade and a half and that increases in urban shares were particularly large in Algeria, Lebanon, and Iraq. (See Table 7.13.) Furthermore, in every country, the pace of urban population growth is well in advance of rural population growth. While emigration has slowed the growth of rural populations in general, only in Lebanon is there evidence of absolute rural decline.

The causes of rapid urban population growth are similar to those in the Third World at large. There are push-pull factors at work that tend to move the population toward urban centers; thus, migration accounts for most of the urban-rural growth differential. Population pressure on scattered areas of arable land and low agricultural productivity serve to drive people from rural areas, while urban advantages and the hope for a better life draw migrants toward the city. Consequently, urban growth is straining government welfare services and the capacity of public utilities to serve the needs of the urban populations; housing, manpower training, and development programs are not keeping abreast of the process of urbanization. The danger in the Middle East is that rapid urbanization will overtax the already stretched administrative resources and urban infrastructures, thus drawing resources needed for development into public assistance programs and present consumption. The economic growth needed to fulfill the hopes of the migrants, therefore, may be in jeopardy in the long run.

SUMMARY

Structural change is occurring in the Middle East, although its past rate and pattern suggest that new institutional arrangements and attitudes are needed if regional development is to be accelerated. Low agricultural productivity provides labor the incentive to migrate to urban centers, yet there is the danger that population inflow plus rapid population growth will inundate urban facilities. The result may be urban stagnation rather than increased welfare. Adverse climate and inelastic supplies of arable land make improvements in agriculture costly, while military requirements drain resources away from development projects. Shortages of human skills and constraints on the innovative spirit have tended to preclude the technological adaptations needed for industrialization, thus impairing the ability to compete in world markets for finished products. The resulting foreign exchange shortages in the nonoil states lessen their ability to import the capital equipment and modern technology needed for economic development. It is against these pernicious difficulties that the new financial power of the oil states should be weighed.

The oil price revolution is providing opportunities for the area that are analogous to those experienced in the sixteenth century in Europe. But petroleum is a finite resource, and in the context of history, the age of oil will be short. When this time of opportunity has passed, will the countries of the region have succeeded in real economic diversification, or will they remain structurally imbalanced, overly dependent on one or two areas of activity and vulnerable to the depredations of rapid population growth? The answer depends in large measure on their ability to establish a greater degree of sustained regional cooperation and cohesion than has been achieved so far.

NOTES

1. T. R. Malthus, Principles of Political Economy, 2d ed. (Reprints of Scarce Works on Political Economy, no. 3) (Tokyo: The International Economic Circle, 1936), pp. 334-35.

2. Ibid.

3. Colin Clark, The Conditions of Economic Progress (London: Macmillan, 1940).

4. Simon Kuznets, "Modern Economic Growth: Findings and Reflections," The American Economic Review 63, no. 3 (June 1973): 247-58.

5. Simon Kuznets, Economic Growth of Nations (Cambridge, Mass.: Harvard University Press, 1971), p. 106.

6. Ibid., p. 211.

7. Ibid., pp. 211-13.

8. Carlo M. Cipolla, The Economic History of World Population (Baltimore: Penguin Books, 1970), p. 92.

9. See, especially, Theodore W. Schultz, "Investment in Human Capital," The American Economic Review 51, no. 1 (March 1961): 1-17.

10. This review of post-1973 manpower movements in the Middle East is based on the findings of Birks and Sinclair of the International Migration Project, Durham University. See, especially, J. S. Birks and C. A. Sinclair, "Manpower and Economic Development: Background, Perspectives and Prospects in the Arab Lands," mimeographed (Durham, N.C.: The International Migration Project, 1977).

11. Yusif A. Sayigh, Entrepreneurs of Lebanon: The Role of the Business Leader in a Developing Economy (Cambridge, Mass.: Harvard University Press, 1962).

12. For a good account of technological innovation in Israel, see Roy Popkin, Technology of Necessity: Scientific and Engineering Development in Israel (New York: Praeger, 1971).

13. Saleh Farid, Top Management in Egypt: Its Structure, Quality, and Problems (Santa Monica, Calif.: The Rand Corporation, 1970).

14. Estimates of urban population are based on United Nations, Statistical Yearbook (1972).

APPENDIX

Assume for simplicity that oil of a single grade is being produced by a state firm and that the short-term marginal cost (MC) is constant up to the full capacity of OX daily barrels. A perceived demand for oil, DD_o, implies that net revenue maximizing output would be OQ daily barrels, where marginal revenue (RR_o) equals marginal cost (OC) at point A. The optimum price would be OP_o. (See Figure A.1.)

But suppose that the national producer is a member of OPEC and that through negotiation and compromise the Conference sets an official price, OP_c. The producer's demand curve then would be $PcBD_o$, as no prospective buyer need pay more per barrel than OPc. Given this kinked demand curve, the producer's marginal revenue schedule would be the discontinuous $PcBER_o$. As the producer would now identify marginal revenue with price, up to point B, there would be an incentive to expand production to OS daily barrels because marginal revenue would exceed marginal cost up to there. Even so, under the prevailing demand and cost conditions, no other price and output combination would yield as much net revenue as OP_o and OQ. Thus, OP_o remains the optimum price, and the national producer could increase net revenue by breaking with OPEC and returning to it. Since support of OPEC's pricing policy implies an economic sacrifice, either the nonpecuniary gains provided by membership more than offset this loss or the capital absorptive capacity of the producer is so limited that it is not interested in revenue maximization.

If demand were to decline, as it did in the world recession of 1974–75, an incentive to cut both price and output would arise. Letting DD_1 represent the reduced demand, the most profitable rate of output would become OT, where marginal cost (OC) equals marginal revenue (RR_1) at point F. The optimal price would now be OP_1. But continued selling at the OPEC price would entail restricting output to OU. Although under actual market conditions, marginal revenue exceeds marginal cost by HK at OU output, output would have to be restricted to this level to avoid excessive inventory accumulation. If the producer were to supply OT barrels at the OPEC price, there would be a daily excess supply of GJ barrels. Thus, the producer has an incentive to increase net revenue by cutting price and expanding production. For most producers, the dissatisfaction with this

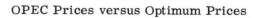

OPEC Prices versus Optimum Prices

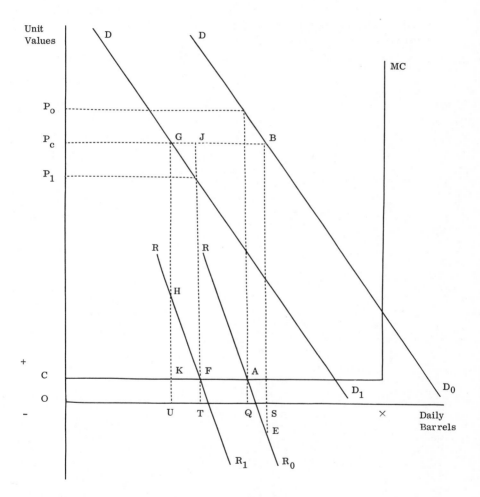

Source: Constructed by the author.

lost opportunity would grow with the passage of time. The argument, of course, is symmetrical. Should demand rise, as it did in the recovery of 1976, individual national producers would have an incentive to raise the price.

The model is useful in tracing the effects of demand shifts upon the motives of individual producers. In general, the greater the difference between a member's optimum price and the OPEC prescribed price, the greater will be the incentive to pursue an independent pricing policy, and the more difficult it will be for the Conference to reach a unanimous decision on prices.

ABOUT THE AUTHOR

DAVID EDENS has been involved in Middle Eastern economic affairs for more than a decade and has served as an economic consultant to the governments of Bahrain, Egypt, and Saudi Arabia. In 1971, he was a Fulbright-Hayes research fellow in the Middle East and, in 1976-77, the Ford Foundation's representative in the Gulf region.

Edens holds a Ph.D. in Economics from the University of Virginia; in 1967-68 he was a postdoctoral fellow in Middle Eastern studies at Princeton University. He has been a member of the Economics faculty of the University of Connecticut since 1962. His publications include contributions to the Middle East Journal and the International Journal of Middle Eastern Studies.